The Corporate Dream

The Corporate Dream

Making It Big in Business

Hank Johnson

A Lyle Stuart Book
Published by Carol Publishing Group

A Lyle Stuart Book
Published by Carol Publishing Group

Editorial Offices
600 Madison Avenue
New York, NY 10022

Sales & Distribution Offices
120 Enterprise Avenue
Secaucus, NJ 07094

In Canada: Musson Book Company
A division of General Publishing Co. Limited
Don Mills, Ontario

Manufactured in the United States of America

Library of Congress Cataloging-in-Publication Data

Johnson, Hank.
    The corporate dream : making it big in business / Hank Johnson.
      p. cm.
    ''A Lyle Stuart book.''
    ISBN 0-8184-0517-1 : $19.95
    1. Success in business—United States—Case studies. 2. Spiegel-
-Case studies. I. Title.
HF5386.J62   1990
650.1'0973—dc20   90-35607
                                      CIP

To my wife Darlene,
my six children,
and my seven grandsons

Acknowledgments

The author wishes to acknowledge the dedication and skills of the entire Spiegel team that made the Dream come true. I also want to thank again the many fine resources that believed enough in our vision to take the risk of joining our effort to create the most beautiful catalog in the world. Last, but not least, my continuing respect and appreciation to our customers, the busy women of America.

Contents

The Corporate Dream

Introduction

The problem with corporate America is that it has lost its ability to dream.

Companies like Ford, IBM, Sears and McDonald's were not built from sophisticated textbook strategies or complex analysis. They didn't become giants by following paths others had forged by coldly calculating risk-reward equations.

Dreams fueled their growth.

Dreams of a new mode of transportation.

Dreams of a business world driven by computers.

Dreams of taking the local general merchandise store national.

Dreams of a clean, well-lighted place that would please the palates and pocketbooks of young, economy-minded families.

Though these dreams may have been born in the minds of a few ingenious men, these men did not keep their dreams to themselves. They shared their visions, and they made their employees part of those visions. They made sure that each employee—from shipping clerks to top executives—understood the basic philosophy behind the company's strategy.

Inspired, motivated, comprehending, those employees responded. Their energy, creativity and enthusiasm were boundless, and they helped set standards that few companies can approach.

Today, corporate realists far outnumber corporate dreamers. For every company like L.L. Bean, Citicorp and Federal Express, there are hundreds of organizations that are unable to lift their noses from the grindstone and see their unique niche in the marketplace.

This book proposes the restoration of the corporate American dream. It is one solution to the problems that plague thousands of this country's companies. The problems can't be minimized. Foreign competition, a wildly cyclical economy, decreasing productivity and quality standards—they are real obstacles that aren't going to disappear overnight.

Many management experts and CEOs have suggested and tried approaches to make the obstacles disappear. Some have been successful. Most have had little impact.

I'm suggesting in this book an alternative to fancy theories and hard-to-implement tactics. As CEO of Spiegel, the catalog marketing company, I had the opportunity to put my strategy into practice. It was the perfect test case. I joined a company that was fast approaching rock bottom. When I left, Spiegel was the country's leading catalog direct marketer and was on its way to becoming a $1 billion company.

The dream was responsible for our success—the dream of a new way of shopping for the busy American woman.

To be honest, not many people—both inside and outside of Spiegel—shared my dream at first. I talked about it with other CEOs I respected, and they all admired my concept but thought it would never work. When I first announced my plans to Spiegel employees, many of them left, saying that they couldn't accept it. The majority of those who remained were skeptical.

All this was to be expected. By definition, dreams are intangible, highly personal things. They can't be analyzed like a balance sheet; they aren't taught in business schools.

But dreams have more power than the almighty silicon chip. And they are America's best natural resource.

Different countries have different advantages in the global marketplace. Some countries have cheap labor. Others have excellent technology infrastructures. Still others have high productivity levels. Our country has the special advantage of unshackled imagination. Our companies have always been pioneers, coming up with revolutionary ideas and creating new products and services. In the past, our diverse corporate cultures have been breeding grounds for innovation.

In recent years, this has not always been the case. Many of our larger corporations seem to be living off old dreams, dreams that have been rendered obsolete by economic, social and technological changes. They have fallen into what I call the "lumpy mattress" syndrome. Once upon a time, that mattress was new; it provided support. Over the years, it sagged and developed lumps. But many people within the corporation found security and comfort in those lumpy mattresses. They resisted any suggestion that the old mattress be replaced.

Companies like International Harvester and General Motors illustrate the perils of sleeping on that lumpy mattress for too long. They didn't wake up to the changes that were occurring all around them.

Change should not be looked upon as an enemy. In fact, change should inspire dreams. Change may be the increasing number of working women. Or it may be the introduction of a new technology. Or it may be the aggressive new posture of a competitor. Or it could be a new consumer purchasing trend.

Whatever it is, change is an opportunity for corporate dreaming.

Where does the dream begin? How it is translated into strategy? Those are two key questions that I'll answer in this book. I'll talk about the formation of the dream—how it evolves, the way it can be refined and the need to obtain corporate-wide acceptance. That last point is critical. At Spiegel, when I announced my strategy for turning around the company, I was besieged with questions like: How are we going to get our sources to sell us these new products? How are we going to get rid of $70 million worth of obsolete products? What tactics can we use to target our new customer?

Those were all good questions. But they paled in significance to the larger question: Does everyone at Spiegel understand and support the dream? Once that question was answered affirmatively, everything else was details. Significant details, certainly, but details nonetheless. I knew that the dream was correct, and when thousands of people shared the same dream, we had the power to turn it into reality.

Turning the dream into reality requires a number of steps, which I'll examine in detail. One of those steps involves leadership. Though I know I'll provoke a great deal of argument on this point, I believe that a dream strategy can't be implemented by an autocratic CEO. The top executive who rules by intimidation rarely succeeds at motivation. A dream can't be forced down people's throats.

Instead, a humanistic approach is called for, an approach that is flexible and flowing, that encourages an open and comfortable work environment. The CEO should ban harsh criticism or black marks for mistakes. Risk-taking should be encouraged, without any punishment for failure. People should talk to one another in a common language, devoid of esoteric statistics and jargon. Obviously, all this has a great deal to do with establishing the proper corporate culture, which I'll discuss.

Throughout this book, I'll refer to the Spiegel model. I'll use other companies' experiences—both positive and negative—to explain certain points, but the Spiegel model will take center stage. There are two reasons for that focus. First, I'm most familiar with the Spiegel story. Second, and more important, an increasing number of companies are finding themselves faced with the same set of circumstances that confronted Spiegel: changing social trends, a declining customer base, outmoded products, an inappropriate corporate culture. Despite this seemingly hopeless situation, we were able to turn a $250 million company into a $1 billion organization in five years. If it could be done at Spiegel, it can be done anywhere.

This is a nuts-and-bolts business book, written for any executive at any organization. It will function on two levels. On the one hand, it's storytelling, describing one of the most successful turnarounds of the last decade. On the other hand, it's a how-to book. Using the Spiegel story as a model, readers will learn how to make their corporate dreams strategic realities.

We live in a business era where the prosaic solutions to problems are frequently ineffective. It's time to try a little poetry. Even the most conservative of business people have dreams. Don't resist them. Don't ignore them simply because they're removed from the humdrum reality of your business.

Let them loose. How? That's what this book is all about.

CHAPTER ONE

A Boy with a Broom

Every dream has a beginning, and mine started long before I arrived at Spiegel.

I wasn't born to be a corporate executive. It took me a long time to get in a position where I could implement and control my dreams. Along the way, however, I picked up precious bits of knowledge. It was knowledge essential to an aspiring corporate dreamer, and I'd like to share with you where and how I acquired it.

A Cabinetmaker's Son

My parents emigrated from Norway, driven from their native land by famine. They settled in the Humboldt Park area of Chicago, an ethnic neighborhood that was home to many Norwegian immigrants. Though both my father and his brother were highly skilled cabinetmakers, they, like many immigrants, worked as unskilled labor when they first came over.

When they arrived, my parents began the process of adapting to a new environment, everything from Americanizing their name (from Johanasen to Johnson) to learning English.

When I was a one-year-old, we moved to the western outskirts of Chicago. My father and uncle, along with another Norwegian, built three bungalows with their own hands. The houses weren't anything fancy—two bedrooms, an outhouse in back—but they were a step up from what we had. Though we were still relatively poor, living in an area where the streets hadn't even been paved, we were moving upward. My father had found a job as a cabinet-maker with the company that produced all the elaborate cabinetry for Walgreen's stores. Back then, drug stores used ornate wooden cabinets, and business was booming, due in no small part to Walgreen's, my father's company's largest customer.

My mother was working as an upstairs maid for the John M. Smythe family, the family that founded the Smythe furniture stores.

Retailing might not have been in my blood, but my parents' jobs certainly made me aware that others had made money in that field.

I remember a number of things from my childhood that shaped who I was to become. First, my parents instilled in me and my two brothers a respect for authority. Though they were strict and believed in discipline, they tempered that belief with love and fair rules.

Second, I recall that, unlike today, play time was unstructured. There were no organized activities available to us. Instead, we created our own amusements. If we saw a movie about pirates, my brothers and I would create a game in which we were pirates. We were forced to use our imaginations to entertain ourselves. We were nothing if not resourceful, transforming trees into ship masts for climbing.

Third, the Depression hit our family as hard—if not harder—than most families. In 1930, when I was ten, our circumstances changed dramatically. My father lost his job (his company went out of business) and a great deal of money in the stock market (he had invested heavily in Walgreen's stock). To make matters worse, my father initially refused to take a job that paid lower than a carpenter's union wage. A staunch union man, he viewed taking such a job as union-busting.

These events exacted a terrible toll on my father and our family. A fiercely proud man, my father never recovered from his losses. Everything he had worked for had vanished, destroyed by a force over which he had no control. In the ensuing years, he drifted away from the family, both physically and emotionally. He moved to Texas, where he found work. But as time passed, his letters came less often, and our family was on its own. We had to go on relief, and my mother was forced to run a cleaning service out of our home to make ends meet.

I grieved for what the Depression had done to my father, how it had managed to take away his self-respect and dignity. But I also learned a hard lesson: you cannot let your dreams be destroyed by events beyond your control. You have to be flexible and adapt to new circumstances. It might be painful and require that you swallow your pride, but that is the only way to keep the dream alive. For all my father's fine qualities, he lacked that flexibility. I would not allow my dreams to suffer the same fate.

Learning About Work

I went to work when I was thirteen. During every spare moment after school, I worked: cutting lawns, delivering newspapers, joining President Roosevelt's WPA program, assisting the school janitor. As the janitor's assistant, one of my responsibilities was sweeping floors. The first day I performed that task, the janitor watched me with an eagle eye. When I was finished, he never watched me again. I handled that broom with the same level of skill with which Wayne Gretzky handles a hockey stick.

It wasn't that I received any great satisfaction from that job. It was simply that my parents had instilled a work ethic in me—a work ethic that demanded I do the best job possible, no matter how trivial the task.

I finished high school with good grades but without the money for a college education. I searched the classified section of the newspaper and saw that Montgomery Ward was hiring for their mailroom. I applied and was soon hired as an office clerk, a euphemism for mailroom boy.

The Wards Mailroom

Montgomery Ward taught me the importance of doing service jobs well. Though sorting the mail and delivering it to various people throughout the company didn't tax my intellectual and creative abilities, I was determined to deliver the mail like I had swept the gym floor: better than anyone else. Instinctively, I knew that the fastest way to get rid of these tasks was to do them perfectly. After a while, someone was bound to say, "That Johnson boy, he's too good to be doing this."

Effie Morris was the one who said it. A no-nonsense executive in charge of Wards' services division, she expressed appreciation for the work I was doing. She appreciated not only my speed and efficiency, but also my personality. She liked that I was courteous and friendly. My parents had taught me to trust my natural instincts, to be myself. Too often, people behave artificially in business situations, straining to be something they're not. It's far easier just to be yourself, to let your good qualities come through.

Effie Morris promoted me to the eighth floor. Though I was still delivering mail, I was now delivering it to the company's top executives.

The House That Sewell Built

Here was my first dream fulfilled. A small dream, perhaps, but not then. It was my first promotion, and I walked through the green-carpeted halls with pride and purpose, wearing my grey linen company jacket, awed by my surroundings. On the eighth floor were the company's top administrative people, Wards' movers and shakers. And on that floor was the legendary Sewell Avery, the man who built Wards. He was tall, grey-haired, and dignified, a 19-year-old's vision of what a CEO should look like.

Mr. Avery was a benevolent despot. Benevolent to the little people, the clerks and secretaries. A despot to the top executives; the more you were paid at Wards, the more likely that Mr. Avery would ride you mercilessly. On many occasions, I would pass by his office and hear his voice thundering behind closed doors, berating executives for one misdeed or another. No question, Mr. Avery inspired terror. When he walked the halls, underlings fled at his approach, certain that he would unleash his bile on them if they tarried too long. Though Mr. Avery was a brilliant financier, most people remember him because of the famous photograph taken during World War II. In the photograph, a grim-faced, defiant Mr. Avery is being carried out of his office by military troops. He refused to deal with the unions, and President Roosevelt had insisted that all companies involved in the war effort must work out a compromise with the unions. When Mr. Avery refused, President Roosevelt sent in the troops.

But Mr. Avery never showed that side of himself to me. In fact, he couldn't have been nicer. When I delivered the mail to his office, he'd often ask me questions: Why was I at Wards? What were my plans? How was I doing?

Mr. Avery's demeanor was in direct contrast to his administrative assistant, a man by the name of Dick Leese. He was a little tyrant who seemed to enjoy pushing people like me around. When I came to Mr. Avery's office to pick something up, Leese would bark, "Wait here!" Mr. Avery, on the other hand, would always ask, "Hank, would you mind waiting for a moment?"

The contrast in styles wasn't lost on me. I despised Mr. Leese's supercilious attitude and greatly appreciated Mr. Avery's courtesy. It was a lesson in management that would prove valuable in years to come.

Perceptions

One day while I was waiting in Mr. Avery's office, he looked at me and said, "Young man, if you're going to get anywhere in the retailing business you have to get into merchandising. That's what makes the business go. You should really try to get into a lower merchandising job here. Why don't you transfer to the sample room? They have jobs there."

Shortly thereafter, I approached my boss, a grey-haired older man named Zelinsky who was just putting in his years. I began by saying, "Mr. Zelinsky, I was talking to Mr. Avery today. . ."

Zelinsky turned white, as if I had invoked the Lord's name in vain. I could see what was going through his mind: I hope the kid didn't say anything that would reflect badly on my department. I related my conversation with Mr. Avery and asked Zelinsky if there was any possibility I could transfer.

A few weeks later, I was transferred to the sample room.

Perception, I was learning, was everything. I had always assumed that to get transferred I would have to go through an elaborate process of forms and requests, that it would take a great deal of time and effort. Zelinsky's perception of my conversation with Mr. Avery circumvented all that. It was as if Mr. Avery had given him a direct order. The culture at Wards ensured overreaction to Mr. Avery's words and deeds. In many cases, the perception of what he wanted was far more powerful than what he actually wanted.

Soon I would experience another example of the power of perception while I was working in the sample room.

I worked in that room for three years, and again "used the broom" better than anyone else. At first, my job involved opening boxes and displaying merchandise. Gradually, they gave me more responsibility. Partly because I worked hard and efficiently—and partly because I understood how things were constructed (thanks to my father)—I was put in charge of the sample room's furniture department.

One day I set up a merchandise review of Wards' unpainted furniture, displaying our furniture alongside Sears' samples. Hundreds of pieces were lined up, like soldiers ready for inspection by the brass. In this case, the brass consisted of Mr. Avery and his vice presidents, as well as various supervisors, buyers and assistant buyers.

The room grew quiet as Mr. Avery strode in, and the first thing he said was, "Hello, Hank, how are you? How are you getting along? Oh, you set this up? Glad to see you're over here."

His words were like magic. With all the bigshots in the room, he was singling me out for attention. If anything could raise my status within Wards, his words were it. From that day on, no one treated me like the wet-behind-the-ears sample room clerk I was.

Absolute Power

But the story doesn't end there. Mr. Avery focused his attention on the unpainted furniture display and, when he finished the review, said in an entirely different tone of voice, "This isn't furniture!" He then turned on his heel and walked out of the room. Based on that one remark, Wards' executives gradually phased out the entire line of unpainted furniture. A line, I might add, that was doing about $20 million worth of business annually.

This taught me another lesson: when authority at the top is too powerful, it weakens the decision-making process all the way down the line. It was absurd to eliminate a $20 million line. When Mr. Avery talked, everyone listened too hard. He never intended to have the products eliminated; he later created a furor when he discovered the overreaction. But his executives were so fearful of doing anything that might run counter to his wishes, they threw commonsense out the window.

An Officer and a Gentleman

In 1942, World War II began, and I joined the air force. Before leaving Wards, I went to see Mr. Wagner, who was the manager of the furniture department. I told him I was going to be a pilot, but that I'd be back. I said, "When I return, I hope you'll consider making me an assistant buyer."

He couldn't very well say no to someone who was going to fight for his country. But neither did he say yes. Though he agreed I had done an excellent job, he added that assistant buyers have a college degree and experience with other stores.

A year later, after getting my wings, I had a ten-day leave and went to see Mr. Wagner again. I walked in wearing my lieutenant's uniform and told him I was going to fly B–17 bombers overseas.

A funny thing happened: Mr. Wagner looked at me like I was a different person, like I was an officer and a gentleman. When I brought up the assistant buyer position, he nodded and said, "When the war's over, you come back and see me." Perception had reared its beautiful head again.

When the war ended and I returned to Wards, I came back to the company as an assistant buyer.

The Cachet of Quality

For the next four years, I learned the ropes of buying. Though I already knew Wards' lines, I had a lot to learn about dealing with sources, negotiating, spotting lines to acquire. I also learned a lesson about quality. Mr. Wagner created a new line of Wards furniture called Hallmark, furniture made from the highest-quality sources. Wards had never offered anything like this, and it was considered precedent-setting; it caused a great deal of jealousy and sniping among our competitors. Ultimately, the line failed because it wasn't merchandised properly, and when Mr. Wagner left the company, Hallmark was discontinued. Still, I saw the excitement and possibilities generated by selling high-quality products. Back then, quality didn't have the same connotations it does now. It wasn't a common word in the vocabulary of manufacturing and marketing executives. Its potential as a selling tool was largely unexplored.

I filed the lesson away for future use and moved on. I was ready for a buyer's position, and a retailing company called Aldens offered me the opportunity.

CHAPTER TWO

Aldens: Flying Solo

When I accepted a job at Aldens as a furniture buyer, it was a small dream come true. Finally, I had the chance to be out there on my own. Like the pilot I was, I'd be flying solo—I'd have a line that was my responsibility. Little did I know that I'd be flying in the same formation for the next twenty-five years.

The Environment

Every starry-eyed dreamer has to grasp corporate realities. When you land that first great job, you often are unprepared for the politics and policies—the culture—of your organization.

I was astonished and disappointed by the political in-fighting that dominated Aldens' culture. Every upper-level manager had carved out his piece of turf, and woe to those who trespassed. When I joined Aldens, they were an $80 million catalog house/retailer that would soon break the $100 million mark. I'm sure they would have become even larger if they hadn't been burdened by some of the most vicious political battles this side of Washington, D.C.

In one corner was Harry Stentiford, a top V.P. of merchandising. Mr. Stentiford was a self-made, up-through-the-ranks guy. To his credit, Mr. Stentiford knew the retail business backwards and forwards and was an expert at playing the political game. To his debit, he was totally unconcerned with the feelings of those who worked for him, and he seemed to delight in changing schedules and putting people down. As my boss's boss, Mr. Stentiford was in a position to make or break my career.

Jack Stahle was another top V.P. Mr. Stahle was the head of operations and personnel (in addition to a number of other titles) and was in many ways similar to Mr. Stentiford. Needless to say, he and Mr. Stentiford despised one another and were constantly at each other's throats. Mr. Stahle also knew the business, and he brought many innovations to the company, especially an enlightened employee benefits policy. But Mr. Stahle was also a tyrannical, vindictive man, prone to fits of temper and paranoia. If you weren't with him, you were against him. He kept a black book that was the bane of his enemies. In it he would note offenses committed by employees, and if you accumulated enough black marks, your career at Aldens was dead-ended.

Bob Jackson was the company's president. A tall, powerfully built man, Mr. Jackson was a hands-off manager. He was above the fray, content to delegate day-to-day operating responsibilities, somewhat removed from the in-fighting. His chief interest seemed to be sports; he had once had a tryout with the Chicago Bears and he still maintained close ties to the sports community. He had risen through Aldens' ranks, starting as a buyer in the shoe department. Despite his lack of involvement with the nitty-gritty details of the business, he had sufficient authority and respect to hold the ship together.

Finally, there was Mark Dalin. A former Wards employee, Mark brought me to Aldens and was my first boss there. Mark was an Ivy League graduate, a tall, distinguished, handsome man in his forties. He came from a wealthy, East Coast, highly cultured family. His manner was formal and reserved, and he was not a skillful political player. He and Mr. Stentiford were opposites; you couldn't find two people who were less alike. Mr. Stentiford recognized Mark's talent, but he resented his background. Mark was one of the golden boys. He had gone through

18

Macy's training program, at the time the most prestigious program in the industry. Mr. Stentiford seemed to take special pleasure in bullying Mark, placing him in uncomfortable situations.

I had a lot to learn. I was dealing with a diverse group of people, a new job and a corporate culture that ran against many of my beliefs. Yet I managed to survive and prosper. Why? How was I able to advance through the political maze and get my programs implemented when other buyers failed to do so?

Because I instinctively knew the first lesson of leadership. I sensed that leadership begins by raising your hand. From the very beginning, my hand was constantly in the air, insistently waving, demanding to be recognized.

A Flair for Ideas

I had more ideas than Campbell's has soups. I wasn't shy about voicing those ideas, and I did so with drama and enthusiasm. But I wasn't a pushy, obnoxious fellow, enthralled by the sound of my own voice, trying to brown-nose the teacher. My ideas and enthusiasm were genuine. I never felt that other Aldens employees resented my attitude. They understood that I loved what I was doing and was excited when I came up with a new or innovative approach.

One new approach involved inserting a swatch of fabric on a page of the catalog. Synthetic leather had just come on the market—leather that looked and felt exactly like the real thing, but cost far less. Leather recliners were very popular at the time. I had a vision of one page of the catalog dominated by a synthetic leather recliner, a piece of the synthetic leather and a price far below what real leather recliners cost.

I shared my vision with my bosses and managed to get Mr. Stentiford to back me. But there were other obstacles. First, Aldens' catalog tended to crowd a page with items, the theory being that more products equals more profits. Second, the page I

19

wanted for the recliner—the back page—belonged to the shoe department; they were a powerful department, since Aldens sold huge quantities of cheap shoes. Third, I was only a buyer; I didn't have the clout to run my idea through the decision-making gauntlet.

Mr. Stentiford's backing helped; there was no love lost between Mr. Stentiford and the shoe department. I knew he'd seize the opportunity to take a page away from the powerful shoe people (Aldens sold more cheap shoes than any other catalog house). But I decided to try and drum up enthusiasm on my own. I contacted Boltoflex, a manufacturer of synthetic leather, and persuaded them to send me a box of ladies' wallets made from synthetic leather. I took those wallets and distributed them to women throughout the company.

The stunt was corny as hell, but it helped sell the concept. We sold a quarter of a million dollars of synthetic leather recliners, a hugely successful item. Pretty soon, all of Aldens' departments wanted to launch similar programs: having one item dominate a page rather than a motley group of items.

I found I had a promotional flair, an ability to come up with innovations and present them in a way that made people sit up and take notice. For instance, carpet tufting machines came into existence when I was a buyer, making it possible to produce nylon carpeting that was cheaper and easier to clean than other types of carpeting. Again, I wanted to give a whole page to the new product. And I came up with a few twists to sell it. First, I hit on the concept of "All sizes, one price." In other words, rather than having a complicated price list that customers had to decipher, they would immediately see one low price: $99.

Second, I suggested to the advertising department that they create a nontraditional spread. Usually, the big carpet companies advertised their product by showing an elegant woman descending a luxuriously carpeted staircase. That's what the advertising department wanted to do. I told them, "Look, we have to sell this nylon carpeting for families with kids and dogs." They came up with an ad that did just that: a picture of a kid watching television, holding a glass of milk and a cookie, and next to him was a huge sheepdog eyeing the cookie; of course, the nylon carpeting was underneath the scene. The headline: "100% Nylon, for families with kids and dogs." Our sales of nylon carpeting tripled.

Every organization has people who develop reputations as "idea men" (or women). These people are irreplaceable and invaluable. Everyone else within the organization serves the idea men. Though an idea man might not be the boss of others, he has the real power. Without him, the organization goes nowhere.

If you aspire to be a corporate dreamer, you've got to start as an idea man. You need the experience of creating ideas, nurturing them, protecting them and helping them grow. You need to find out why some ideas fail and some succeed.

Believe me, not all of my ideas worked. But I began to learn how to increase the odds that they'd make it. I learned how to give them a fighting chance.

Just as important, my status as an idea man led to more opportunities. I was given the freedom and responsibility to come up with bigger ideas. In any organization, idea men get promoted faster than others. I was no exception to that rule.

Winning in a No-Win Situation

In a typical political power play, Harry Stentiford was able to wrest control of the hardline division of Aldens' retail store chain from the retail department. Shortly thereafter, Mr. Stentiford called me into his office and told me he was impressed by my work and wanted to put me in charge of hardlines at those stores. He made me a manager, gave me a plush new office and created a new position for me.

It was an offer I couldn't refuse. With hindsight, though, it might have been best to do just that. For one thing, Aldens' stores were a losing proposition—they were "junior" department stores, miniature versions of stores like Gimbel's. They had no real niche in the marketplace. In addition, I was dependent on buyers who weren't under my direct authority. The way my position was set up, I wasn't their boss.

I did everything possible to make the retail stores successful. I closed unprofitable departments. I set up an incentive program for buyers so that they'd give priority to my lines. For four years, I fought an uphill battle, trying to lure customers away from competitors like Wards and Sears, who could beat me on quality, price and selection.

Ultimately, I lost. Mr. Stentiford called me into his office and said, "We're eliminating your job. It hasn't really worked out." He gave me the choice of being demoted back to a buyer for the stores or the catalog. "Or," he said, "you can leave Aldens."

I told him I'd take the buyer's job with the stores. But I didn't leave it at that. He was implying that I was at fault for the stores' continuing slide, and I just couldn't accept that implication. "I want you to know that I didn't ask for this job," I said. "You created the position, and I've done a good job for you. You can demote me, but you can't blame me."

Perhaps it wasn't good form for a junior executive to criticize his boss. Yet I was sure Mr. Stentiford was wrong. I suppose I was taking a risk. But it was a bigger risk to say nothing: Mr. Stentiford would have always thought of me as the guy who let him down. Perception is everything, and Mr. Stentiford had the wrong perception.

A funny thing happened. After I defended myself, Mr. Stentiford's attitude changed. In fact, he actually apologized to me! He agreed I had done an excellent job and that economic factors were responsible for the reorganization that eliminated my position.

Another lesson learned: Always speak up when you feel you've been unfairly treated. If you're right—and your boss is sufficiently open-minded—you'll earn his respect.

Mr. Stentiford respected me. I know that because of what happened a few months later. Through his deft political maneuverings, Mr. Stentiford had managed to seize control of Aldens' advertising department. He immediately installed Mark Dalin, my former boss, as advertising vice president and gave me Mark's job as manager of home furnishings.

It was a position of real power, and from that point on, my career at Aldens took off.

The Catalog Experiment

Based on my experiences with the nylon carpeting and synthetic leather recliner, I was convinced that catalogs didn't have to be all things to all people. The idea of targeting markets, presenting one or two great products with drama and flair, appealed to me. I decided to take that idea to its logical conclusion.

What if we created a new type of catalog? Something people had never seen before? It would be larger than other catalogs. It would make extensive use of color. Each page would spotlight a few items rather than many. We'd come out with a special catalog for hardlines, one that would give even prosaic items like tires full-color treatment and pizzazz.

Every bone in my body told me the time was right for a tabloid-sized catalog. And I was just as sure that if I didn't present the idea properly, Mr. Stentiford would turn it down. By this time I had learned that a great idea wasn't enough; you had to garner support and participation from the people with the power to make it happen.

I had also learned to approach different people in different ways. What would work with Mr. Stentiford? Well, I knew better than to outline the concept in all its detail. If you gave Mr. Stentiford too much information, he'd always find fault with some aspect of an idea and shoot it down. Therefore, I carefully mapped out a two-stage campaign.

The first stage involved "teasing" him with the idea. I went into his office and said my group was working on a concept that would allow us to present hardlines in a better way at less cost and give us the opportunity to pull in a great deal of cooperative advertising from our sources.

"How are you going to do that?" he asked, obviously intrigued.

"I can't tell you everything right now," I said, explaining we still had some loose ends to tie up. "But the advertising people have been very cooperative."

That last statement was intended to get his competitive juices flowing; Mr. Stentiford had recently taken over control of the advertising department and wanted to demonstrate his power to set their agenda.

"We don't want to explain the idea in detail to anyone except you," I told him. I suggested that if he could make a special concession and come in on a Saturday morning, we'd provide him with a formal presentation.

I was fashioning a favorable environment. First, I was giving him the chance to take credit; if no other top executive was aware of what we were doing, he had the opportunity to be its sole sponsor. Second, I was turning the presentation into a special event. By calling for a Saturday meeting, I was clearly communicating that the idea merited a private, uninterrupted session.

Saturday came, as did Mr. Stentiford, and we pulled out all the stops. My group put on a presentation with all the bells and whistles. We played to Mr. Stentiford's ego, talking to him as if he were the president of Aldens. I knew very well that my boss thought of himself as the rightful heir to the throne; he believed his power and knowledge entitled him to be treated like the president.

Mr. Stentiford bought the concept. He subsequently presented the idea to Bob Jackson. Though I wasn't there, I heard he said something to the effect of "My boys came up with an idea that's pretty darn good. I went in last Saturday and worked with them. You'll like it. It's going to be exciting."

It was. Our new tabloid catalog took customers and the industry by storm. For the first time in Aldens' history, we were perceived as innovators. Sales jumped and other catalogs quickly followed our lead.

And for this corporate dreamer, it was a classic example of how to buck the odds and make things work.

If You Were Your Boss. . .

Some people have the knack of getting along with everyone. They make friends, not enemies, up and down the line. It's one of the most valuable skills a corporate dreamer can have; you'll find very few CEOs who are despised or who have left a trail of dead bodies in their climb to the top. It's a myth that most of the powerful executives in corporate America are ruthless dictators. The top CEOs who really accomplish things have countless friends who helped them along the way.

What's the secret? Well, my secret was to put myself in their shoes. I asked myself what Mr. Stentiford's concerns were? What time was best to approach Mr. Jackson with a proposal? What problems were of concern to Mr. Stahle?

I learned to think as they thought, to feel as they felt. It wasn't always an easy process, but it worked. For many Aldens employees, Jack Stahle was an especially difficult person to work with. It didn't take much for him to mark you down in his black book; even the most innocuous remark could set him off. I couldn't afford to have him as an enemy; I had just been promoted to junior vice president. As head of operations, Mr. Stahle had the power to bottleneck all my pet projects.

After about a month as V.P., I was called into a meeting with Jackson, Stahle and the company's treasurer. They were discussing a proposal to toughen credit terms for Aldens' customers, and I objected, saying that I worried about what tougher credit would do to sales. Mr. Jackson decided it would be wise to stall a decision on the subject until after we analyzed the effect the plan would have on sales.

A few minutes after the meeting ended, I received a call from Mr. Stahle's secretary, informing me that he would like to see me in his office. Instinctively, I knew something was wrong. I went into his office and said, "Do we have a problem, Jack?"

He looked at me as if I had crawled out of the sewer. His face turned beet red, and he hissed, "You crossed me! What did you have to open your mouth for? I had it all set!"

I was aghast. I had no idea that the credit plan was his baby. In that moment, I saw all my years of hard work at Aldens going down the drain.

"I'm so upset with you," he thundered, "that I don't even know if I can continue to work with you."

There was only one thing to do. I knew that if I tried to defend my position, Mr. Stahle would eat me alive. So I put myself in Mr. Stahle's place: What could I do to defuse the situation? The answer was absolute, hat-in-hand humility.

I said, "Jack, I want to tell you something right now. I worked very hard for fifteen years to get the job I have. I know you had to approve my promotion. It's impossible for me to think that I would purposely do anything at a meeting with Bob Jackson and other officers that would in any way put you down. I'm a junior vice president, and for me to oppose the most powerful guy in the company would be ridiculous."

When I finished my mea culpa, Mr. Stahle was a different person. It was as if the incident had never happened. From that day on, I never had another major problem with Mr. Stahle. Incidentally, the credit terms were tightened only slightly. A compromise had been struck, and Mr. Stahle saved face and I made my life much easier.

The point of this story isn't that you have to go around humbling yourself to get ahead. Though it was called for in this instance, other people require other approaches. The point is that you have to see things through their eyes and react accordingly.

The worst thing I could have done was engage in a shouting match with Mr. Stahle. It would have put my dreams in jeopardy. Uncontrolled confrontation should be avoided at all costs. In any company, personalities and politics lead to these confrontations. Everyone reading this book has witnessed them. No one wins. They create such animosity that people cease to work together productively.

I don't think I made a single enemy in my twenty-five years at Aldens. In fact, I learned something from every person I worked with. Sometimes, I learned what not to do; Mr. Stahle and Mr. Stentiford gave me vivid lessons about management styles that struck me as counterproductive. But there was also a positive side to the learning experience.

Mark Dalin, my first, boss, taught me how to act in business and social situations. Because of my working-class background, I had a lot of rough edges that needed smoothing. By observing Mark, I discovered how to smooth them. Mark took me to plays and concerts, taught me how to order in fancy restaurants, gave me a crash course in various social graces. In other words, he helped me become comfortable dealing with a different class of people, a different world than one I had been accustomed to. A CEO must have the ability to relate to a wide range of people, to talk to them on different levels. Through Mark, I acquired that ability.

Communicate, Encourage and Motivate

As I moved up through Aldens' ranks, I developed my own style of management. In many ways, that style was a reflection of my personality: honest, enthusiastic, open, motivational, optimistic, communicative. From the very beginning, when I was in charge of Aldens' home furnishings department, I endeavored to create an esprit de corps. I never played favorites. Instead, I communicated to my people that we were in this together; that if our department did well, everyone in the department would do well. I encouraged everyone to have fun at what they were doing. I wanted my people to like their jobs. If there's a problem, tell me. If you have a solution, no matter how off-the-wall it might appear, tell me that too.

I figured that if I could avoid the tension and backbiting that marked so many departments in Aldens, I'd give us an edge. If I could get my group to want to be better than any other group, then it would be a self-fulfilling prophecy.

On the other hand, I set certain limits. I wasn't a soft touch. In my department there were rules and you had to abide by them. If someone broke the rules, I could come down hard. But if I took someone to task, I didn't do it in a way that humiliated him. For instance, I always used the pronoun, "we": "How could we do such a thing! This can never happen again! We have to think better next time."

I never carried a grudge. When someone left my office after one of these sessions, everything was back to normal. I'd see him in the hallway and talk to him as if nothing had happened.

The result was that we functioned as a team. I know that's an overused word, but it's the best way to say it. We all pulled together toward a common goal. My groups constantly outperformed other groups in the company. It wasn't because I was so much smarter than any of the other managers, or that I had any special advantages. I simply got more out of my people than anyone else.

The End of the Line

Eventually, all my bosses left Aldens: Stentiford, Jackson, Stahle and Dalin all went on to other things. The company was sold to Burt Gamble, chairman of the Gamble Skogmo stores, who brought in Carle Wunderlich to be president. Though Carle had many good qualities as an administrator, he didn't know the catalog business. He was willing, therefore, to let me run things as the number two guy, giving me the title of executive vice president.

Under our combined leadership, Aldens prospered. I did everything possible to rid the company of the divisive politics that had impeded its progress. Gradually, I molded Aldens into one big team, and profits rose accordingly.

Yet I wasn't content. Because of what I had accomplished— and because I wanted to accomplish even more—I asked to be named president. On a plane ride to New York, I broached the subject with Carle. I suggested that Carle become chairman and CEO and give the president's title to me.

"No way," he said. "Chairman doesn't mean anything. President is the important title here. If you want to leave, you can."

I strongly expressed my disappointment to him.

"If you're not comfortable," he said, "why don't you take one of those other jobs you've been offered."

Carle was well aware that I had been contacted by other companies and had turned down a number of attractive positions. It so happened that I had just received an offer from Avon, an offer that would double my salary, give me the security of a five-year contract and numerous other perks.

It's hard to leave a company after twenty-five years. But I had no choice. I still had dreams—dreams that I couldn't realize if I remained in my position at Aldens. So I accepted the Avon offer, little realizing that it would be a steppingstone to something beyond my wildest dreams.

CHAPTER THREE

Avon: Testing Leadership

For the first time, I would be CEO. I was excited about putting my ideas into action. I had dreams of building a business at Aldens, but it had been impossible to implement my ideas there. Avon, however, was a fresh start.

As part of a diversification plan, Avon had launched a direct marketing division to sell non-Avon products to customers without face-to-face selling. It was an excellent strategy, capitalizing on the equity in the Avon name.

The opportunity to head this arm of the cosmetics giant promised much. Avon had grand plans for its new division, setting $100 million in sales as a short-term objective.

When I arrived, the new division was only two years old. They had sent mailings to lists of potential customers and were receiving a 7 percent response rate (responses are either product orders or inquiries about the product). I was astonished. In the direct response business, a 2 percent response rate is good. When you receive a 7 percent response to a cold list, either you have the greatest offer in the world or something isn't right. I decided to investigate.

You Can't Get Something for Nothing

A look at the books turned up problems. In the first two years of the division's operation, they had boosted sales to $8 million annually. Losses, however, were $10 million each year.

I visited the division's new and elaborate computer operation in Virginia. I asked to see an order. The computer people showed me a print-out of an order for ladies' slacks. The customer had ordered all colors of a low-priced line—$6.99 per slacks—but had not yet paid for her order.

A little more investigative work revealed the woman was responding to one of the many free-trial offers the division was running. Typically, Avon sent the order and invoiced it in thirty days. The problem was that thousands of their customers weren't paying their bills and weren't sending their purchases back. Avon didn't have a collection system in place to prevent this from happening.

I immediately curtailed the free-trial offers and insisted we only take checks and credit card payments. I told Avon that these actions would result in a sales nosedive, but it was necessary. There was no point in getting terrific response if we were losing millions of dollars a year.

Shaping Up and Cutting Back

I brought my division back to reality. I began with a speech: "Listen, folks, we're not Avon, that big, rich company. We're a crummy little company called Fashions by Avon. As soon as we understand that we're this tiny division and act like it, we'll get things under control and be able to move forward."

By reducing our division's payroll by two-thirds, I was able to cut our losses dramatically. At the same time, I hired a few key people who understood the direct marketing business. Prior to my arrival, Avon was attempting to run their direct marketing arm without sufficient direct marketing expertise.

In meetings with my managers, I explained that we were going to become a catalog business, operating within Avon's culture. But I emphasized that we had to build the company on our own. Certainly there were advantages to being part of Avon, but we couldn't ride on Avon's coattails.

I was acutely aware of the downside of existing as a small part of a big organization. It's all too easy to become spoiled, dependent on the free flow of cash and other resources that are available. Too often, big companies acquire small ones under the assumption that an infusion of cash will help the smaller entity achieve its growth potential. In reality, the acquired company becomes complacent, always looking to the parent for help.

For those reasons, I wanted Fashions by Avon to exist as a stand-alone company and to grow on self-generated cash. In a little less than two years, we were well on our way toward that goal. We produced a nice catalog that achieved the industry standard 2 percent response rate, and we began to establish our niche.

Our niche in the marketplace and within Avon were two different things. In a way, the latter effort was more difficult, given the contrast between Avon's culture and my business philosophy.

The Arrogance of Bigness

Until the 1974 recession, Avon was a company that could do no wrong. Everything they touched seemed to turn to gold, and the investment community loved them.

They didn't love them, however, when the recession hit and Avon was caught flat-footed. For years, Avon had launched programs every month for their representatives, allowing them to sell Avon merchandise at discounted prices. It was akin to having a sale every month, and each new program dramatically boosted sales. In the early seventies, the frequency of these programs increased, going from once a month to once every three weeks to once every two weeks. With each increase in frequency, sales rose significantly.

But you can't have constant sales indefinitely. When the economy went flat, so did Avon's sales. Suddenly, Avon was no longer the darling of the investment community. The stock price plummeted from a high of 100 to 19.

I came to Avon in the middle of that decline. The reaction of Avon employees can best be described by one word: shock. No one believed it could happen there. Many employees had participated in the company's stock option plan, and with alarming speed some of them went from being paper millionaires to being in the hole.

Avon was a company that spent money lavishly. Expense was no object when it came to employee travel, dining and lodging. The benefits and compensation policies were just about the best in the business. Their solution to problems was to throw money at them, as if a sufficiently large expenditure could solve anything. Avon had signed the biggest real estate lease in the history of New York at the time of the stock decline, and they were left with an albatross of half-empty offices.

No question, Avon was a great place to work. It was like a wonderful country club, and it was extremely rare that anyone was kicked out. But it was excessive, and Avon was a victim of its excesses. The darling of Wall Street, they weren't prepared to deal with adversity. When the bottom fell out, they didn't know what to do.

Avon was a great company, with many talented people. Their culture fostered the idea that there was only one way to do things: the Avon way. If Avon needed an aircraft carrier, they would say, ''Tom, you, Harry and Mary build us one'' rather than looking to outside experts like Newport News Shipbuilding who had the experience. Change came hard at Avon.

As Avon's fortunes continued to decline, they attempted to diversify, which was the right strategy. But Avon didn't bring much common sense to their diversification efforts. They still were an insular, inbred organization with little sense of any market other than their own. Despite the stock downturn, they overspent as they attempted to diversify.

Few if any of their diversification efforts worked. I remember suggesting that Avon should sign Jimmy Connors and Chris Evert, then the reigning king and queen of tennis, to long-term sponsorship contracts. Avon refused to do so. There was no clear-cut reason for their refusal except that "it wasn't the sort of thing Avon did."

Avon clung to the security blanket of the familiar. They continued to run the same advertising they had run for years, characterized by the Avon lady with the familiar "ding-dong, Avon calling" theme. I think they were hoping against hope that everything would return to normal, that their present difficulties were an aberration and if they patiently waited everything would be fine.

But it just didn't happen.

The Lesson of Change

More than anything else, my experiences at Avon taught me about the necessity of change. As soon as Avon's stock began to nosedive, the top executives should have realized that a new direction needed to be forged and followed. A new dream had to be created.

Avon possessed numerous assets. Not only were they still generating a great deal of cash, but the Avon name and sales force were powerful tools. They needed to capitalize on those tools.

I suggested one possible direction. Why not build a network of salespeople located within America's largest corporations? I was aware that time was becoming an increasingly high priority among working women. What if Avon rented space within various corporations' offices, selling Avon products to employees during office hours?

My suggestion was met with little enthusiasm. It was too radical a departure for Avon; they just couldn't see the big picture. But their marketplace was changing. No longer would most women welcome Avon representatives into their homes. A rapidly increasing percentage of women were joining the work force, having neither the time nor the inclination to entertain sales representatives in their homes. In addition, this was a time when an increasing number of women were moving into large apartment buildings where security factors prevented Avon representatives from gaining easy access to potential customers.

Avon helped me become aware of the changing nature of women's purchasing needs and their priorities. That knowledge would be very useful in my next job.

An Organization or an Institution?

Avon also taught me that an organization, no matter how large, is not necessarily an institution.

Avon was not an institution because there was too much softness in the character of the company. An institution has a strong vision of the future and its place in it. Avon lacked this vision; they weren't willing to change with the changing times in order to preserve and expand their market.

There was also a lack of employee motivation. Or rather, employees were motivated by money and little else. Though it might not have been a conscious decision, Avon had bought its employees' loyalty. An institution, on the other hand, doesn't need to rely on such tactics.

I realized I wanted to build or be part of an institution. It wasn't enough to be part of a large organization, no matter how prestigious or profitable. My satisfaction would come from helping construct something that would last, something with roots and an inspirational, motivational business philosophy.

I wanted to work for a company where everyone was enthusiastically working toward the same goal, striving to create something new and better.

Being in Charge

As president of Avon's direct marketing division, it was my first opportunity to be in charge, both in title and in fact. I found that it suited me. I enjoyed the responsibility and accountability, setting policy, motivating people, redirecting their philosophy.

But my opportunity to do these things within Avon's culture was limited. I would be able to achieve only so much and no more. After a year and a half, I was restless. Though I had set my division in the right direction and we were growing, I was alert to other possibilities.

Unbenownst to me, Spiegel was conducting a search for a new CEO. When I received a call telling me they wanted to interview me for the job, I expressed interest. When I received an offer, I sat down with Avon's president and told him about it.

I began by saying that I felt a responsibility to finish the job I started at Avon, and if he wanted me to turn down the offer, I would. Though I wanted to accept it, my sense of loyalty forced me to give Avon's president the chance to keep me.

"No," he said. "I think you should consider it. It seems right for you."

I expected his reaction. I had been an outspoken critic of Avon's culture, which had not set well with certain executives. I sensed that they perceived me as an outsider and that it would be better for both of us if I left.

Though I was disappointed to leave my job at Avon unfinished, I was excited about Spiegel. Though I was aware Spiegel

was experiencing problems far worse than Avon's, I was confident that I could help the company overcome them.

My vision for Spiegel hadn't yet crystallized; I needed to learn
more about the organization as well as outside, marketplace
forces. But I saw a great opportunity. I was attuned to the trends
in catalogs and the changing role of women, and I sensed that a
catalog that appealed to affluent, busy women would be a terrific
niche marketing strategy.

So I left Avon and joined Spiegel, my dream for my new
company already starting to take shape.

CHAPTER FOUR

The Inspiration

Corporate dreams don't just happen. You don't wake up in the middle of the night and cry, "I've got it!" Instead, they evolve over time. They come to life gradually, responding to things observed and experienced.

That brings us to the first rule of corporate dreaming:

Rule 1: Be a Keen Observer of Trends

All dreams have a source. That source is not only the small, isolated world of your organization or industry. It is the combination of trends, cultural attitudes, and economic changes that affect society.

Long before I joined Spiegel, I was aware that the marketplace was changing. I noted the progress women were making: I would have had to be blind to ignore such things as the Equal Rights Amendment, the feminist movement, the increasing number of women occupying positions of power within government and industry, the growing number of women with advanced degrees. I suspected that a new class of working women was emerging—professional women needing fashionable clothes but having little time to shop.

There were other trends: department stores bowing to union and equal-opportunity pressures and replacing informed salespeople with less knowledgeable clerks; the gas crisis, causing many people to curtail their use of cars; the growing consumer demand for quality products.

It struck me that working women, with less time and more money, would make excellent catalog customers. If a catalog were created with that specific market in mind—a catalog that reflected the fashion-conciousness of this audience—it would be enormously successful.

It was a great dream. When I arrived at Spiegel, I found an organization where I could translate the dream to strategy.

Rule 2: Dreams Often Work Best in the Worst Environments

It is difficult, if not impossible, to implement a corporate dream strategy in an organization that is flush with success. If you've just had a dream year, new dreams become superfluous.

Ideally, you'll be part of an organization that needs and is ready to make dramatic changes.

When I came to Spiegel in 1976 as CEO, I was coming to a general-merchandise catalog house that wasn't the ideal: although they needed to make dramatic changes, they weren't ready to make them.

The managers running the company knew only one approach to the business, and that was the traditional Spiegel way. Never mind that profits were nonexistent and sales had been stuck at $250 million for years. They trusted in the status quo and were adamant at not changing their tried-and-true strategy: selling low-priced goods to relatively low-income customers through a catalog that had all the style of the telephone directory.

Prior to my arrival, the consulting firm of Booz Allen Hamilton had conducted a study for Spiegel's owners, the Beneficial Finance Corporation. That study gave the company three options: 1. Sell the company. (But they added it was doubtful anyone would buy it.) 2. Liquidate the company. (The problem with this option was that it would require a $200 million write-off, not a feasible alternative in those days.) 3. Find an outsider who could come in and do something different with the company.

I was that outsider. Spiegel's owners had conducted an extensive search for a new CEO. Not only were they looking for someone who knew the catalog business, but a leader-manager who could save the company. When Beneficial hired me, however, I'm not sure they really understood the radical repositioning I was contemplating.

I knew what I was up against: competitors such as Sears, Wards and J.C. Penney with far more resources than Spiegel; a group of managers who would be highly resistant to any change in philosophy or strategy; an anachronistic catalog operation. My friends in the business advised me that though they knew my intentions were good, my heart was in the wrong place—nothing could save Spiegel.

But all these obstacles were small compared to my dream. I knew the catalog business. I knew that the business was ready for something different. For years, catalog marketers had plodded along, taking a utilitarian approach to the market: give the people what they want. Catalog companies assumed their customers wanted variety, credit and inexpensive goods. All the catalogs reflected this strategy. Everyone followed Sears' lead, assuming that if it was good for Sears, it was good for everyone else. No one had a distinctive image or style.

Spiegel was worse than most. In a sense, they weren't a seller of goods; they were a seller of credit. In the fifties and sixties, this had worked. It doesn't take a genius to see that if you borrowed at 5 percent and received 18 percent on receivables, you were going to make money. But inflation cut those margins and Spiegel was still giving easy credit to anyone and everyone.

Still, they knew how to produce catalogs and fill orders, and they had a recognizable name. That was all I cared about. As long as they had the physical capabilities to produce a catalog, I was in business.

Rule 3: Dream of a New Niche

The corporate dreamer should not worry about being the biggest; he should be concerned about being the best. The best in one particular field.

In other words, be a realistic dreamer. If I had dreamed of challenging Sears for its leadership position, I would have failed; their resources were too great, their lead too long. I instead targeted my dream and scaled it down to size. This strategy had precedents. George Romney, when he was the head of American Motors, manufactured a small car called the Rambler that was tremendously successful. Rather than competing head-on with the Big Three automakers, he created a unique market for his company.

Look for your niche. Search for a market the bigger companies have overlooked or decided was too small. Or discover a market that is emerging, that the market leader can't hit as fast as you can.

If you have great plans for your company, be sure you're not imitating a larger competitor. Consider an overlooked demographic group. Spot a coming trend. Create a new product or service. The one thing corporate dreamers have going for them is imagination. Imagine a customer you can make your own, one specific sort of person with well-defined life-style and characteristics.

I imagined a woman in her thirties, an ad agency executive with two children, a lawyer husband and a condo in the city. In the past, this woman probably would have been home taking care of the kids, returning to the work force much later in life. Now, she and her husband were each putting in fifty-hour workweeks. This woman was acutely aware of the clothing she wore, the brand names of high-ticket products she bought. She wanted to make the right purchases, but she wasn't about to waste hours shopping at stores to find the things she wanted. To her, if the brand name was right, if the price was reasonable, if buying it was a relatively painless process, she was sold.

Rule 4: Be Prepared for Dream-Breakers

During my first few months at Spiegel, virtually everyone thought I was crazy. Or if not crazy, seriously deluded.

To some extent, I didn't blame them. I didn't try to be diplomatic. Right from the start, I held individual and group meetings in which I said Spiegel was heading for a cliff, and if we didn't change direction, we'd go over the edge. I emphasized that we had to find unique opportunities—"Uniquely Spiegel" became my constant refrain.

I told them to forget our current customers, to discard our present catalog. I said we had to go after a market that currently wasn't buying from catalogs, but a market that I was sure would buy from them in the future. They would come to believe that catalog shopping was the smart way to shop.

In the beginning, no one was on my side. More than one Spiegel executive told me why my plan was doomed to failure. In time, three-quarters of those executives left the company. A common complaint among those who left was, "I'm too old for this." As soon as they said that, I knew they didn't have any place in the dream. It wasn't that they were too old—I was fifty-six when I came to Spiegel—but too inflexible.

Corporate dreamers must have thick skins. You can't let naysayers discourage you. Dreams are threatening to those who have lost the capacity to dream. Those people will respond negatively. Roll with their punches and keep fighting for what you believe in.

Rule 5: Be a Charismatic Communicator

You want people to embrace your dream as though it were their own. If you merely explain the dream—if you only show employees charts and strategic plans—it will never happen. You have to be an actor, delivering passionate orations about what the future holds.

I was an evangelist when I came to Spiegel, hawking my dream like a preacher on the stump. I never missed an opportunity to paint a picture of what Spiegel could be if they embraced my vision. I talked about how we were going to be on the leading edge of catalog marketing, about how we were going to do something that had never been attempted before. I stressed that all Spiegel employees were going to be part of the most exciting business venture of their lives.

Time and time again, I preached the Gospel of Spiegel according to Hank Johnson. I stirred up our buyers, getting them to share my fantasy of dealing with upscale sources, designer names and high-ticket products. When talking to our list people, I romanced the coming computer era, telling them we would purchase the best equipment and train them to use it.

Most important of all, I gave them a taste of the future. Understanding changing attitudes toward fashion was crucial. In the past, it took at least one year for a fashion to make its way across the country; it would start on the coasts and gradually make its way toward the heartland. Television was rapidly accelerating this pace. With the assistance of the mass media, new fashion trends were instantly communicated to and embraced by the entire country. Wearing fashionable clothes and purchasing fashionable products were going to be of paramount importance to our customers.

With a glow in my eye and a quaver in my voice, I proclaimed that we were going to be there, catalog in hand, ready to serve this new catalog customer.

Like a politician or pitchman trying to make memorable points, I used buzz words to convey my message. When talking about our catalog, I said it would be a ''fine department store in print.'' I wanted everyone in the company talking and thinking this way.

The point of these verbal exercises was to get them to believe. That is the war any corporate dreamer has to win. Employees who merely go through the motions—performing their jobs competently but routinely—cannot execute a dream strategy.

If hundreds or thousands of employees believe in the dream, their enthusiasm is communicated to others. It makes it far easier to sell that dream to outsiders—to consumers, the media and product sources. It becomes a self-fulfilling prophecy.

Showmanship is essential. Certainly as CEO you have much more freedom to pitch your dream. But any manager can do it, even if it's only in a presentation to the boss.

It might seem like an undignified approach. Not everyone can play the part of inspirational leader. But you won't find many dull, by-the-numbers bureaucrats advocating corporate dreams.

Rule 6: Shake Things Up

You have to convince the company that your dream is more than words. How? By demonstrating that things are going to change.

This doesn't mean firing a bunch of employees or issuing edicts about the company's new direction. It does mean taking some action that will rouse the company out of its lethargy, something that will quickly show them that you mean what you say.

I hired an advertising manager whose approach was diametrically opposed to what Spiegel people were accustomed to. He was an arty type, concerned with colors and lighting, eager to experiment and innovate. He wasn't a disciplined person, and I figured he wouldn't last long; the catalog business requires discipline, adherence to schedules and formats. Still, I wanted to hire someone who would break the link with the past. When I hired this guy, people knew I was serious about changing the company.

One of the first assignments I gave him was to shoot catalog photos with ''wrinkles.'' Spiegel catalogs traditionally used static studio shots of models whose clothes never had even a suggestion of a wrinkle. This was accepted catalog procedure; you wanted everything to look perfect.

I didn't. I asked him to find different photographers who would shoot on location, and to make sure the models he used looked "real"—windblown hair, different expressions and, yes, an occasional wrinkle in their clothing.

No question, this shook up the company. I had given a job of importance to someone who was as out of place at Spiegel as Queen Elizabeth at a wrestling match. Suddenly, everyone knew I was serious about putting my dream into practice.

Rule 7: Clear the Decision-Making Decks

The best way to water down a dream is with layers of management. Show me an organization with a grab bag of titles and I'll show you an organization that is death to corporate dreams.

Flat line management is the opposite of the traditional pyramid structure, eliminating the numerous titles at the top (executive vice presidents, senior vice presidents, etc.) and consolidating decision-making among key executives. It ensures fast decisions, few misunderstandings and quick implementation.

Instead of scores of vice presidents, I substituted just seven vice presidents, each with line responsibilities and each reporting directly to me. I made myself CEO and president.

Certainly this wasn't a popular move, especially among the executive and senior vice presidents who were being demoted in title if not in fact. Perhaps all those titles and specialized jobs are necessary in an organization that is pursuing a more conservative strategy. But they were antithetical to my purposes. My worst fear was that I would try to communicate a plan of action, and that plan would be misinterpreted as it filtered down through the bureaucratic structure. I feared I would give instructions to one vice president who would communicate those instructions to three others who would pass it along to five group managers who would convey it to fifteen other managers, ad infinitum. By the time it reached the people who would actually carry out the task I wanted, my original meaning would be woefully distorted.

I also delegated responsibility down to the lowest possible levels. In many companies, you need a prestigious title to make decisions. Unfortunately, the people with the fancy titles often lack the necessary information to make the right decisions.

When I did this, the lower-level employees were appreciative. It made them feel empowered, a part of my grand design. They were suddenly entrusted with authority they never had before.

Rule 8: Don't Throw Out the Equity with the Bathwater

As much as I wanted to change Spiegel, I didn't want to be perceived as an anarchist. I didn't want to create the impression that I was rejecting everything that Spiegel was. It's one thing to be looked upon as a reformer. It's another thing to be viewed as a radical.

So I attempted to forge a link with Spiegel's past. The name, after all, had equity, and it would have been foolish to divorce myself totally from its inherent value.

That was one of the reasons that I asked the president of the company, Ted Spiegel, to stay—not as president, but as vice president of marketing. This was a critical job—more than anything else, we had to change our public image. I knew that Ted not only knew the business, but he was intelligent and perceptive. And, of course, he was a Spiegel.

At first, Ted was reluctant to accept my offer. For one thing, he would have to give up his presidency. For another, my ideas certainly clashed with the Spiegel tradition. Third, his father, who was a past chairman of the company, advised him to refuse my offer. But I told Ted that if he took the job, he would have more fun in the next ten years than he ever had as president. I'm sure Ted didn't have complete confidence in what I was trying to do, but he decided to take a chance on me.

His decision to remain was important. It was a small victory, but a victory nonetheless. Although I still hadn't won any converts, at least I had some potential allies.

Lessons to Be Learned

At this point, you might wonder how all this applies to you. After all, the situation at Spiegel was probably different than the one you face. If you don't come into a company as CEO with carte blanche to make the changes you feel are necessary, what relevance does this have?

The relevance is that all dream strategies share certain problems, tactics and opportunities—certain rules—and the Spiegel story illustrates them. In this chapter, we've talked about the first stage of the dream strategy. No matter what your dream might be or what position you occupy within an organization, you'll encounter situations similar to what I encountered at Spiegel.

You may be a division manager who sees an opportunity for a new product line.

You may be a vice president who has the ear of the CEO; you may be able to garner his support in forging a new direction for the organization.

You may even be a junior executive with a dream. Perhaps you don't have the power necessary to implement it, but you can start whispering in a more powerful executive's ear and get the ball rolling.

In each case, you've looked beyond your business to the world outside and spotted something: a social trend, changing buying habits, a growing new market, a technological breakthrough. You've anticipated the impact of what you've observed, and you've formulated a strategic dream around it.

You're going to need a niche to turn that dream into reality.

You're going to have to fight internal resistance to your vision.

You'll need to communicate your dream with great gusto and eloquence to drum up support.

You'll have to shake things up.

The way you do all these things might be different than how I did them at Spiegel. Your position, your organization and your dream should all be considered in your approach.

We've concentrated on the first steps to take in launching the dream. Next, we'll focus on some of the obstacles you'll encounter, and how to overcome them.

CHAPTER FIVE

Preparing for Action

Inspiration fuels corporate dreams. But along with that inspiration, there has to be perspiration. A substantial amount of sweat equity is required to get dreams off the ground.

At Spiegel, we did a lot of sweating, especially at the beginning. The task before us was enormous: we were going to make huge changes not only in our catalog, but also in our customer base. To understand our first steps, you have to understand what the catalog business was like in 1976.

The Marketing Environment

Back then, there were far fewer catalogs than exist today. The big three were Sears, Montgomery Ward and J.C. Penney, followed by Spiegel and Aldens. A handful of specialty catalogs—Lillian Vernon and L.L. Bean being the most prominent—also had small slices of the market. A number of department stores weren't really in the catalog business, but they sent Christmas books to store patrons.

The catalogs all looked pretty much alike in that undeveloped market. Catalogs were still a shopping source for people who lived in rural areas or who didn't have stores nearby. Most of the products featured were utilitarian: ready-to-wear clothes, automobile parts, housewares, tools. The great irony of the situation was that the Big Three catalog companies weren't really catalog companies; they were retailers first, and catalogs were secondary marketing tools.

In short, the catalog industry was stagnant; innovation was virtually nonexistent. It was the perfect marketing environment for a dreamer. A conservative thinker might look at the market and say, "It's a nongrowth industry; nothing's happening, and nothing's going to happen." A corporate dreamer, however, will think, "There's an opportunity no one else is capitalizing on; the market is ready for change."

When I joined Spiegel, I recognized the need for change. But I also recognized there were different routes for change.

We could change the type of merchandise we sold. Perhaps we could give up our ready-to-wear business and concentrate on hardlines. We might be able to get by if we became a home furnishings catalog. Or we could concentrate on new strategies for going after our customer base, trying to be more efficient and effective in our marketing efforts.

Upon reflection, I was convinced those alternatives were only piecemeal solutions. They might increase Spiegel's profitability, but they offered no chance at greatness. We'd still be no better than fourth on the totem pole, forever trailing Sears, Wards and Penney.

There had to be another way.

Open Your Eyes

I didn't rely on research studies to find that other way. I did what every corporate dreamer should do: I opened my eyes and looked around. Here's what I saw.

I saw that computers were going to become an increasingly important part of our business. Computers meant information, and for direct marketers information is crucial. Computers would allow us to do a better job of tracking our customers, segmenting them, determining their buying preferences. It would make target marketing a reality for catalogers. I wanted to target the working woman, and I instinctively knew that computers would facilitate that effort.

I saw the 800 toll-free number coming into existence. Back then, toll-free numbers seemed mysterious and intimidating, and people were wary of the concept. Yet I suspected it was only a matter of time before it became an accepted part of the direct marketing business. AT&T was spending millions of dollars publicizing and promoting toll-free numbers. Once Americans caught on that there was no gimmick—that they could make free, long distance calls—it would have a dramatic impact on our business. It would make ordering from a catalog a faster, less expensive, more personal process. With the right type of catalog, we would be in a position to capitalize on toll-free numbers.

I saw the emergence of the working women—more women than ever before were pursuing careers, including those who were wives and mothers. I've talked about this in a previous chapter. No doubt, this was the single most important development that caught my attention.

And I saw the need for change. In 1976, most businesses labored under the illusion that conservative, maintenance strategies were wise. Taiwan, Japan and Korea were relatively insignificant specks in the global marketplace. Inflation was still a rumor. Baby boomers were just emerging from their countercultural isolation. Old boy networks flourished, and the status quo appeared permanent.

But just below the calm surface, major economic, technological, social and cultural forces were roiling. You'd notice them if you visited foreign countries or if you heeded the warnings of researchers or read news reports of the giant strides being made in the computer industry.

It would have been easy to ignore or dismiss these changes, to assume that they wouldn't have an impact on our company and industry.

But every corporate dreamer must embrace change. Since the late seventies, the rate of change has accelerated. There are many more changes on the horizon. If you can attach your dream to one of those changes, you'll greatly increase the odds of success in your favor.

The dreamer is different and embraces change.

One Step at a Time

I made no secret of my desire to make changes at Spiegel. When Spiegel's parent company, Beneficial Finance, talked to me about the CEO position, I clearly communicated the need for change. As part of our deal, I received carte blanche to do what I saw fit. As long as I didn't lose significant sums of money, I could turn the company upside down and inside out.

Which is what I did. But I did it gradually. It would have been foolish to remake Spiegel overnight. You can't go from a down-scale, me-too catalog to an upscale, unique one in weeks or months. In fact, I told the company owners that the process would take five years.

Time is absolutely essential for corporate dreamers. As much as you might want to, you can't implement all the facets of the dream immediately. You have to let it unfold over time, testing different aspects of it, letting it evolve.

From a practical standpoint, the question becomes: What do you do first? You have to create the concept and communicate it internally—that comes before anything else. Then you have to make some small, significant moves to support what you've been communicating.

At Spiegel, one of the first things I did was move our offices from the Near West Side of Chicago. We resided in an old, decrepit warehouse. It was a dreary, dusty place in an industrial area, more appropriate for a manufacturer of widgets than the company I wanted Spiegel to become.

We found a building in Oakbrook, a suburban area that was attracting innovative growth companies. It was a hassle to move; it was expensive and logistically difficult. But the move was worth the trouble.

You see, I believe that the personality of a company comes from within. The image you present to your market, to your suppliers, to your employees, to your customers, starts inside the company. It's not all about brick and mortar, but if your working environment contradicts your corporate philosophy, you're in trouble. How was I going to motivate my people in such a depressing building? How could I talk about a new, upscale catalog when we were surrounded by old, low-rent facilities? How was I going to recruit the type of employee I wanted to a run-down office building?

So we moved. We left a lot behind, both literally and figuratively. I instructed our people to bring only what they could carry; we were buying everything else new. We created an office that symbolized the new Spiegel philosophy. No office had doors. Not mine, not anyone's. The core of the building was elevators, washrooms and meeting rooms. The rest was open areas and partitioned office spaces. The result was a feeling of flexibility and communication. It was an office built for growth and change.

Crawl Before You Walk

I didn't want anyone trying to be a hero. I didn't want a ready-to-wear buyer to become so wrapped up in the dream that she junked all the present merchandise and replaced it with $500 suits and $200 shoes. Sure, that was our ultimate goal. But we couldn't alienate all our old Spiegel customers. We needed to phase them out, along with inappropriate merchandise, over time. There had to be a transition period. If we tried to make the dream happen immediately, we'd be out of business.

So I looked for practical ways to begin the changes. There was a "Hot Merchandise" book that Spiegel sent annually. It was designed to whet appetites for selected Spiegel items, and Spiegel had been sending it for years. The first week on the job, I learned that they were about to mail 24 million books.

I met with the outgoing chairman of Spiegel and insisted they cut that number to 10 million. I did so for two reasons. First, I recognized that they were sending the books in a scattershot pattern, based on the belief that the more they sent, the greater the response. I figured that by cutting the list, we'd save a lot of money, and most of the people they were mailing to weren't the type of customers I wanted for Spiegel.

Second, and more important, I wanted to create waves. I was delivering a message: things are going to change. By exercising my authority, I communicated that I was in charge and that I was empowered to act. Corporate dreamers not only require power, they need to foster the perception of power. Otherwise, their directives will be ignored or will not be taken seriously.

I was serious about changing Spiegel. When word spread that I was cutting the mailing list, my decision created an uproar. More than one person grumbled that "the guy is telling us what to do and he hasn't even been working here a week."

They hadn't seen anything yet. I called the Spiegel management group together—the president and a number of vice presidents. I told them about the changes I envisioned and that it meant we would be eliminating most of our product lines.

They were shocked.

The merchandise vice president said, "You're not talking about our $5.99 ladies polyester pants, are you? We do $5 million worth of business there."

"Yes," I said. "There's a much bigger market out there that we're missing."

"You're not talking about our two hundred order stores, are you?" the operations vice president asked.

"Yes," I responded. "I'm thinking of getting rid of them."

"But we do 40 percent of our business out of them," he responded.

Forty percent of the wrong kind of business, I silently added.

But I made my point. I wanted everyone to understand that our traditional customers were a vanishing species and our product lines were dated. Our old customers would find other marketers better equipped to meet their needs. To cling to long-standing product lines was suicidal. No matter how much income they generated, those product lines had no future; they would produce less and less income with each passing month.

Recruiting Potential Stars

One of my first tasks was to replace people who had left shortly after my arrival. We started recruiting. We were looking for special people. We couldn't afford heavyweights, and given Spiegel's troubles, we weren't likely to attract them. Instead, we sought individuals with specific retail or catalog skills who could get excited about Spiegel's new direction and who believed in it.

Getting the right type of merchandising people was critical. We started hiring young, senior buyers from department stores. Though they didn't know anything about the catalog business, we quickly taught them. These buyers had contacts with sources we didn't have, with manufacturers of upscale, fashionable merchandise.

More often than not, the buyers we brought in were women in their early thirties, well educated and ambitious. They were good communicators, related well to other people and saw the job as a great opportunity. They were confident decision-makers with a superior sense of fashion. We started a program of growing our own future stars. We hired bright, young, motivated people right out of college, people who loved the idea of our new Spiegel.

Slowly but surely, this type of employee ceased to be the odd woman out. After a year, the majority of Spiegel employees believed in my dream, and they had the knowledge and desire to help make it happen.

The Search for Quality

Changing the catalog wasn't going to be easy. We couldn't simply toss out all the old merchandise and bring in new lines in every department. We'd lose money hand over fist if we tried it, and I'd promised the owners I wouldn't lose money.

Yet we had to start the process. Although our goal was to target an entirely new customer base, we had to keep our old customers buying, at least for a while. It was a tricky proposition. Where and how could we start?

I began by making sure that all our people knew what we were building toward: becoming the ultimate, convenient way of shopping for the fashion-conscious women in the demographic upper third of households in the country. I stressed that the operative adjective in front of women was "busy." "She has the money but not the time." I reiterated. "She knows what she wants, but between her job and home life doesn't have the hours to spare to get it."

The old Spiegel catalog wouldn't appeal to that woman. What were the simplest things we could do to the catalog to give it that appeal without alienating our old customers?

Well, everyone likes to shop in a freshly painted store. Why not "paint" the catalog? Painting meant more color. It meant doing away with the amateurish line drawings of kids in the children's section. It meant shooting photos on location with new, high-speed cameras and taking out the old, stodgy studio shots of frozen models.

Most of all, it meant taking a hard, long look at our catalog merchandise and gradually junking the stuff that had no place in our future.

It was a traumatic process, and it started with our planning meetings. In the past, buyers were excluded from these meetings;

the premise was that high-level decisions about merchandise could only be made by high-level people. No more! I insisted buyers and assistant buyers be included in the decision-making process. They had to be motivated, involved. I wanted them to be like me when I was at Aldens; I hoped they'd try to make their department the best one in the company.

At our planning meeting, we went over every single catalog product with an eye toward our future customer. Typically, our conversations would go like this: "Mr. Johnson," the buyer said, "I know what you want to do but we can't. I know you want to get rid of our $3.99 blouses, but we do $2 million worth of business in those blouses."

I responded, "Okay, we'll keep it for this year, but next year they only go in our sale book. Find something better at a higher price, and we'll replace it with that."

Part of the process involved eliminating our lowest-priced products and replacing them with higher-quality, more expensive merchandise. We knew that certain lines were of poor quality and that they were frequently returned for that reason. Those products were the first to go.

But price and quality weren't our only considerations. It was a question of fashionable products versus utilitarian ones. We decided if a product was purely functional—if it didn't have a fashionable appeal to it—we didn't want it. That meant no more automobile tailpipes and cheap carpets. It meant that if we carried a toaster, it couldn't be just any toaster; it had to be a toaster with a special design or a unique accessory—something that would attract the interest of our target audience of working women.

In that first year, we implemented our phase-out/replacement plan for all catalog merchandise. Combined with our graphic makeover, the Spiegel catalog changed. The changes were subtle; they weren't so pronounced that our old customers felt they were being ignored.

But we were testing the waters and preparing ourselves for more sweeping changes. Somewhere out there were women who couldn't care less about a $3.99 blouse, but who did care a great deal about quality brands and designer fashions. I could visualize those women carrying the Spiegel catalog around with the same pride as they would a Gucci bag.

We were still a long way from that vision. But with our initial changes, we could see where we were heading.

CHAPTER SIX

The Balancing Act

During the first few years of putting any dream strategy into action, you're walking a tightrope. Lean too far to the left or right and the dream shatters.

How was I going to get three hundred key employees to walk the line? The new people I had brought in wanted to charge forward; they were ready for a revolution. The veteran Spiegel people were cautious; most of them thought change should come at a snail's pace.

Some executives accepted the dream intellectually, but didn't really believe in it. Others believed in it, but didn't understand how we could make it work without going bankrupt. And there were a few who thought I was just plain crazy.

It was time to convert the masses.

Preaching to Whoever Would Listen

What could I say to turn the atheists and agnostics into believers? My talks usually went along these lines:

"Why should we be the lowest man on the totem pole, always looking up at Sears, Wards and Penneys? Our survival depends on our doing something different. Let's accept we're dead ducks if we don't do something different.

"Be with me! Forget for a moment whether you believe in the dream. Simply accept that we need one. You've got to believe we need one. We can't go on the way we have.

"The dream is logical. Everyone is overlooking a tremendous, growing audience of working women. No catalog company is meeting her needs. There's no law that says that all catalogs have to be the same. Look at magazines; they're not all supermarket tabloids. There's a magazine for every type of demographic and pyschographic. The same is true for stores, clubs, restaurants.

"Why not catalogs? Why can't we create something different?"

I'd meet with the different departments and translate the dream for them, explaining what they could do to make it a reality.

I'd go to the advertising department and say, "You can be the leaders in the industry, the point people, ahead of everyone else. Okay, we have low-income customers now. But a beautiful store is admired by all demographics. Even a department store basement can be nice. So first thing, let's look at our store."

Pulling out a catalog, I'd point to some godawful page, maybe a "superstar value" showing a leisure suit made of "rich, woven polyester." Well, everything about it was tacky and low-class; polyester was the cheapest material around and the presentation had all the quality of a carnival barker's spiel. "Look at this, do you think this looks like a department store? You think the woman we're targeting is going to buy this?"

I insisted that we had to stop doing these things. It's going to take a while before all our merchandise is high-quality, I admitted. But the least we could do is start presenting the merchandise we had in a more attractive light. The time will come when quality is the single most important word in marketing, I predicted. We have to prepare ourselves in advance for that time.

We worked toward that goal, making the transition from a black and white to an all-color catalog, phasing out utilitarian merchandise and improving the "look" of our book.

Synchronized Movement

The key thing was pace. If we went too slowly, we'd never reach our goals. If we went too quickly, we'd alienate all our old customers before we acquired new ones and thus we'd lack the financial base to go on.

I wanted everyone moving at the same speed. "It's like a football kickoff," was my refrain. "No offsides penalties, everyone moving downfield together and closing in on the same goal at the same time."

At first, everyone's actions didn't conform to the metaphor. We'd have our planning meetings, and I'd get everyone excited about making changes. I waited for our merchandising people to bring in new lines, our advertising people to make dramatic improvements in catalog quality, our customer service staff to institute new policies.

And nothing would happen. In many cases, I found that managers were hedging their bets. The buyers, for instance, would leave planning meetings with stars in their eyes; they couldn't wait to make things happen. Their bosses, however, would pull back on their reins, urging caution.

I'd sit down with the managers and ask, "Why aren't we moving forward?"

"Well," they'd say, "it's too risky. We think it's not appropriate yet."

"Yet," I'd respond. "That's a big word. Yet. Yet is now. Let's get moving."

An even more difficult problem was those who wanted to remake the catalog overnight. I loved their enthusiasm and hated to hold them back. But we couldn't afford significant failures. They'd find a top-quality manufacturer and want to buy their most exotic line, hoping to devote an entire catalog page to it.

Again, I'd sit down with the go-getters and say, "I don't want to disappoint you, but we're not ready for this. You know what will happen? We'll take a whole page, and we'll all be thrilled that we pulled it off. What will happen when it doesn't sell? You'll want to drop the line. Here's a source we'd love to have four years from now. But we won't have him, 'cause we dumped him. Even worse, it'll get around the industry. Other sources will be wary of us.

"How about if we try a different approach with these 'quality' sources. Let's avoid being market creators. Instead, let's pick their best-selling line, not the most expensive or most fashionable line. See, we're going to have to keep that line whether it sells or not. Because next season, or the one after it, we'll be drawing new customers who will buy it."

There's no set timetable for a dream strategy. Each organization will have to determine how long they'll need to unfold the strategy in all its facets. Some might require a year or two. Others, five or even ten years.

But everyone has to have a timetable, and every employee in the company must be working at the same pace. It's going to be tempting for the people who must believe in the dream to throw caution to the winds and try to do everything at once. It's likely that the skeptics will drag their feet.

You can't allow that to happen. If it does, the dream's core will be fragmented. You'll be sending mixed messages internally and externally. People will wonder if you really have the dream under control, if you really know what you're doing.

From a practical standpoint, that means investors—owners, boards of directors, stockholders—will be skeptical; they might pull the plug prematurely. There will be tension among your people, fights over how fast or slow to go.

The media, industry and financial analysts will lose confidence; they'll talk about how you can't manage the strategy properly.

To prevent this from happening, you need to monitor the rate of change. Set the pace, and as soon as you see stragglers or sprinters, get them back in line. Don't wait. The quicker you react, the easier it is to control the organization's movement.

The Elusive Customer

The customer I wanted for Spiegel was clear in my mind. I knew how she dressed, what movies she enjoyed, how her house was furnished, the brand names that appealed to her. I could sketch her profile with unerring accuracy.

Every dream strategist visualizes his dream customers. They become obsessions. Your goal is to know them better than they know themselves. With that knowledge, you're in a good position to go out and find them. The search isn't easy. But at least you know what you're looking for.

At Spiegel, I was depending on my marketing vice president, to lead the search. I made it clear to him that we had to go beyond the traditional catalog customer lists. A large percentage of our target market had never even bought from a catalog before, and we had to find some way to locate them.

We were breaking new ground. At the time, the catalog industry was unsophisticated in prospecting and defining its customer base. Other catalog companies believed that "more is better": flood the market with mailings on the assumption that the more you mail, the more likely you'll be to find that one-in-a-hundred customer.

Ted Spiegel and I took a different approach. We obtained detailed census tract information, and Ted divided the populace into seven distinct demographic groups. Using a number of factors—including education, income and home value levels—we categorized our present customers into the seven demographic groups. To our dismay, we found that 80 percent of our customers were in the lowest three groups.

That had to change. We needed to reverse the ratio. I envisioned a time when 80 percent of our customers would be in the top three groups.

To help us achieve that goal, we hired a well-known New York direct-response agency to create ads to run in women's magazines, ads designed to bring us new Spiegel shoppers.

Unfortunately, their approach was all wrong. Their thinking was traditional direct response: test, test and test again. The ads were all incentives and offers, designed to generate responses. Although getting responses was certainly a goal, it was putting the cart before the horse. We needed to create a new image for Spiegel, a new style. No ad that put offers before image would reach our target audience; they wouldn't understand what the new Spiegel was all about.

We then found a general advertising agency, Marsteller in Chicago, who had a great deal of experience in advertising packaged goods—in building brands, in shaping attitudes toward and awareness about a product. Their advertising worked. A series of ads positioned Spiegel as a fine department store in print, communicating to working women that our catalog was the best place for them to do their shopping.

Perhaps the smartest thing we did was create a mailing list unlike any catalog list. We went after people who had never bought from a catalog before—a precedent-setting approach. Our marketing team began compiling names of relatively affluent working women.

What were we going to send to these potential new customers? We decided upon "Discover Spiegel," a preview catalog designed to entice them with good values on our best merchandise. We did everything possible to make Discover Spiegel a reflection of what we hoped to become. We put our best products in it, and we cut our prices as low as we possibly could. We also made sure the preview catalog looked good—the graphics, layout and paper stock were the best we could afford.

We couldn't have asked for a better response. Despite the fact that we still didn't have all the types of products that we wanted (we still were burdened with a great deal of middle-of-the-road or lower-end merchandise), thousands of new customers came into the fold.

Initially, the success of our Discover Spiegel mailings was more psychological than financial. After the mailings, we had our first tangible proof that an audience for the new Spiegel was out there. They were so hungry for our type of catalog that they could overlook our bargain-basement image and the uneven quality of our products. Throughout the organization, people cheered. Success wasn't guaranteed. But at least it seemed more likely now than it had for years.

The Order Stores

Spiegel's order stores accounted for 40 percent of our business. After our customers ordered products, many of them picked up their merchandise at these stores (rather than receiving them at home). When I decided we were going to close them, everyone was horrified. Actually, that's an understatement. Some of my top people thought closing those stores might be the beginning of the end.

They didn't think we could survive when we cut off that limb of our operation; we'd lose too much too quickly. I respected their opinion, and I listened to the arguments against the cut. It was estimated we'd lose $50 million, that we couldn't make up for that loss if new customers kept coming in at their present pace, that closing the order stores would have a negative impact on employee morale.

Those arguments made sense. But the arguments for closing the stores were stronger.

First, the order stores were serving our lowest demographic groups. Virtually every one was located in the worst part of town.

In two or three years, order-store customers wouldn't be with us anyway; why postpone the inevitable?

Second, they were a financial time bomb. Most of the order-store customers bought on low-end credit. Credit was granted through a byzantine structure of in-store credit managers, and I suspected we were giving credit to people who shouldn't get it. That scared me. I wanted to get my hands around our receivables, to bring them under control. I couldn't do that while our order stores were operating.

Third, the order-store delivery system was inefficient. I won't go into the complex logistics. It's enough to know that much of order-store profit was lost to the mechanics of assembling orders.

If we closed the order stores, I figured we'd be closer to my goal of converting most of our customers to toll-free ordering. We'd immediately upgrade our demographic base. And we'd save operating costs—we had 1,600 people employed by our stores.

I recognized this was a sensitive issue, and I didn't simply issue a decree mandating the closing. Instead, I brought the issue out into the open and encouraged discussion and debate. Again, I took to the stump, making my arguments in large groups and small ones. The last thing I wanted was to create the perception that I was acting arbitrarily and unilaterally. Everyone might not agree with what I was doing, but at least they'd understand my reasons for doing it.

In 1979, we began closing the stores. No question, it hurt us. Right off the bat, we lost 10 percent of our customers. In the next year or two, we lost many more.

But it was worth it. Bloodless revolutions are rare. Some people are going to be hurt. It's unfortunate, but it can't be helped. We had to jettison parts of our past, and the order stores simply had to go. It was a risk. For a while, the tightrope I talked about earlier got pretty wobbly. But we made it across to the other end. Free of our order stores, we were in a far better position to move forward.

Turning a Tough Corner

All the actions we took during those first few years had an impact. I can't pinpoint the exact day or week the change occurred, but it was like magic. Suddenly, we were pointed in the right direction.

I'm not talking from a financial or even a merchandising standpoint; we still had a long way to go in those areas. No, I'm talking about how John the advertising guy and Mary the buyer felt about the company. No longer were people walking around with long faces. No longer were people openly questioning Spiegel's fate and wondering if the place would be open when they came to work. No longer were people sending out resumes, desperately searching for other jobs.

The majority of Spiegel employees believed. They believed we had a chance, not only of surviving, but of prospering. For a while many of them were willing only to give me the benefit of a doubt. Now, they were willing to give a lot more.

They'd seen the start of the turnaround with their own eyes. They'd watched and participated in the beginning steps of Spiegel's transformation. We'd been able to make major moves without going under. We'd brought in new merchandise, spiffed up the catalog, targeted new customers, closed the order stores.

Lo and behold, despite the doomsayers, we had survived.

You could see the change in the way veteran Spiegel people went about their jobs. It was as if they'd been reborn. The excitement the new, young employees brought to their jobs rubbed off. The veterans hadn't been challenged for years, and after the initial shock wore off, they were glad to be challenged, to have a goal to work toward.

You could hear the change just by listening to conversations as you walked through the offices. Nobody was sitting around silently shuffling papers. They weren't wasting time talking about what they were going to do when they got off of work. Instead, they were debating and discussing new sources, shouting out new ideas for the catalog, trooping into an executive's office with a layout, their faces flushed with excitement. The energy was palpable. These people liked what they were doing.

Too often, management drowns itself in detail and ignores the emotional impact of a new strategy. They get wrapped up in how to make it happen rather than in who will make it happen. You see it with all the mergers and acquisitions, the leveraged buyouts and spinoffs. After these dramatic changes sweep through a company, employee morale is lower than a worm in the gutter. Most employees feel left out, overlooked. No one has taken the time to involve them in the new company.

Implementing a dream strategy means major changes. The way employees react to those changes is critical. You can't expect people to embrace and carry out the dream without assistance. You have to pay attention to their needs, their concerns. Sure, they have to understand what you're trying to do. But even more important, they must be emotionally involved. They can't be allowed to distance themselves from the corporation's success and failures. They've got to invest part of themselves in the organization. That happened at Spiegel. Much of what I did in those early years was designed to make it happen.

You can talk all you want about how a company is going to change. But people have to see the change for themselves, to know they're part of it.

One of my favorite metaphors involved comparing Spiegel to a ship. I told everyone that when I arrived, the ship was foundering in dangerous waters. Every day, someone would jump overboard.

"What we've done so far," I'd say, "is pull the ship into the wind. The wind's at our bow, the ship's steady and under control, and now we can gradually move toward our destination. We're not there yet, but if we all pull together, we'll reach a wonderful new land."

CHAPTER SEVEN

Transition: Getting the Goods

The heart of Spiegel's dream strategy was the merchandise we wanted to sell. No matter how many other changes we made, if we couldn't conspicuously change the kind of products featured in our store, we wouldn't have a chance.

On the surface, it seems like a simple thing. If you want products that appeal to upscale working women, you go out and buy them from upscale sources.

There were only two problems with that logic. The sources didn't want to sell to us, and our buyers didn't want to purchase from them.

Those were big problems.

The Source Mentality

The upscale sources we wanted to buy from—the classy brand names and makers of fine private-label goods—had a number of reasons for not wanting to sell to Spiegel.

They maintained they didn't sell their merchandise in catalogs.

Based on the old Spiegel image, they felt that we wouldn't reach their market.

They were also worried about jeopardizing their relationships with their primary customers, major department stores.

At the time, sources had "exclusive" deals with many of their customers. One source would only sell to stores like Marshall Field's or other top-level retailers. Another source would only sell to mid-level stores. Some stores insisted that if a source sold to a low-level store like Goldblatt's, they wouldn't buy from that same source.

That's why many sources were wary of giving us any merchandise. They feared the reactions of their "discriminating" customers.

The Buyer Mentality

Many of our buyers were equally resistant. They just didn't want to part with their old sources.

That might seem strange, in light of all the talking I had done to involve them in the dream. You'd think they'd understand that if we were to survive, we absolutely had to develop new sources.

But I had been a buyer. I understood the special relationships buyers develop with sources over the years. It was one thing to embrace the dream's concept. It was something else to implement it.

You see, the buyer-source relationships were more than business. They'd been buying from these men and women for years, and they'd established friendships, comfort levels.

The other problem was that some of the buyers were lazy. They liked placing the same order year after year; it made their jobs easier. They didn't have to worry about overstock because they'd simply run the same merchandise in the next catalog.

Starting the Dance

I wasn't naïve. I knew that changing the buyers' and sources' mentalities was going to take time. The key was to make the change as painless as possible.

I likened the process to going to a dance. I know how difficult it is to get up your nerve to ask someone to dance. You approach her, hat in hand and heart in your throat, and then she says, "I'm not dancing this one." There's nothing more deflating to the ego.

At the same time, I also know what it's like to go into a supper club with my wife and hear a band playing and see a deserted dance floor. I say to her, "Let's dance," and she says, "But there's no one out there." Still, I convince her to give it a whirl. Seconds after we're dancing, another couple joins us, and then another. Soon, the dance floor is packed.

Our buyers had to go through the same process. They had to get up the nerve to talk to new sources, deal with rejection, and keep at it until the first one said yes and the others followed.

What could I do to make it easier for the buyers to sashay up to a new source?

I started with a role-playing suggestion. Imagine, I said, that you're buying for Marshall Field's. Think about the lines, brands and designers you'd have. Sit down and make a list. Go out and learn who are the finest makers of women's blouses (or men's shirts or coffee cups or whatever). Find out who are the quality sources for non-branded, private label items for Field's, Neiman Marcus, Lord & Taylor.

I continued: Now make another list next to that one. On this list, put our sources. For both lists, arrange the sources according to price point and quality.

Our buyers examined the parallel columns and saw the lowest price point on the department store list was the highest one on the Spiegel list.

I told them to go after that source. As soon as I said it, I could hear them breathe great signs of relief. I wasn't asking them to do the impossible. The bottom rung on the department store list was possible for them to reach, or at least for them to conceive of reaching. It was only one level up from their current sources.

My strategy was simple. Once they got that new source, we'd drop the lowest one from the Spiegel list. I'd then assign them to go after a source that was one rung above the source they had just acquired. Once they got it, I'd drop another one from our list. It was a neat series of moves that would allow us to change gradually, remaining profitable during the transition period. Add a higher-quality source, subtract a lower-quality one.

The reality, of course, was a little more complicated. The buyers' first trips to higher quality resources were traumatic. Their established sources treated them like royalty. When they called upon a new source, however, they often found themselves sitting in waiting rooms. And when they were finally ushered in, they didn't get to meet with a vice president. Instead, they were sitting across a desk from a salesperson.

It was difficult. I heard the same story time and again. "Get a commitment from Source A," Source B would say, "and I'll take a chance on you." Source B, of course, said the same thing about Source A.

But I told the buyers to be persistent, to keep knocking on the same doors and talk about our dream. In many instances, we'd send a vice president along with them on a second or third visit.

During this initial period, the frustration levels were high. The buyers had a tough time cracking the nuts. They needed a tool that would give them leverage. A tool that would demonstrate to the resources what placing their merchandise in the Spiegel catalog would do for them.

The Layer Cake

Imagine a three-layer cake in the shape of the United States. Each layer represents one-third of the U.S. in demographic divisions. On top of the cake are candles placed at major department store locations throughout the country—Macy's, Dayton-Hudson, Neiman Marcus, and so on.

We gave a picture of this cake to all our buyers and explained how they could use it to convince sources that our dream was right in line with their objectives. The buyers loved the tool and proceeded to use it to whet the appetites of sources for increased profits.

A buyer would take the picture out and say to a source, "Look the top third of the cake controls 60 percent of all discretionary income. That's the layer all your department store outlets claim they're targeting.

"But take a good look at the cake! Their method of selling goes right down through the bottom two layers. Their stores are open to everyone. They advertise in newspapers that everyone reads, not just the top demographic group.

"Now consider what Spiegel is doing. We give you a national market—you can see from the candles that you're missing huge sections of the country. The department stores are located in the major cities. It used to be that most of the top third layer was located in or close to the major cities. But that's changing. The high-tech revolution and other factors are causing a population shift away from the big, industrial cities. Women in suburban and exurban markets are gaining tremendous purchasing power.

"You do most of your national advertising with the big department stores, but their advertising goes straight through the three layers. Spiegel's advertising, on the other hand, goes directly to your target market.

"In the next five years, we'll corner your market."

It was a powerful selling tool. Suddenly, resources understood our dream. Many of them gazed upon our cake and said, "If it works, it's a great idea."

The Psychological Shift

We were making progress. In my first four years at Spiegel, we had made significant change in every area.

But we still had a long way to go. By 1980, we were caught in a transition period. Neither the low-quality Spiegel of the past nor the high-quality Spiegel of the future, the company was struggling to define itself—not only to our customers, the media and the industry, but to ourselves.

This was especially true for the buyers. They had successfully eliminated many of our low-end sources, discarding merchandise like tires and other products that didn't fit in. Many of their new lines were profitable, and it was tempting to dig in and bask in our moderate success.

But we couldn't be content with that, and I did everything possible to ensure that our buyers were also not too satisfied.

"You're in charge of your part of the store," I'd say to a buyer. "If you've got a great new source, if you want more room to display the merchandise, ask for it. If you can demonstrate it's worth it, we will give you six pages, ten pages, whatever it takes."

The buyers constantly had to evaluate their sources. Sure, they were selling $3 million worth of work wear. But they needed gradually to eliminate those overalls from the catalog, since our future audience of affluent working women weren't going to walk into their corner offices looking like farmhands. The same went for the six-way suits we purchased for next to nothing from the Orient. All of it had to go, and the buyers had to replace that merchandise with better quality goods.

Much of the selection process was subjective; it would have been much easier if there were some manual that listed exactly what merchandise Spiegel should sell, a manual that allowed them to pick and choose. The buyers had to rely on their instincts, on their knowledge of where we were in the total strategy and where we wanted to be.

All dream strategies have a midpoint, and we'd reached ours. The danger of the midpoint is complacency. You've reached some objectives—objectives that seemed unreachable a few years back—and you instinctively want to consolidate your gains, to take a breather.

The problem is that a dream strategy is like an airplane in flight: when it stalls, it starts to dive. You need to maintain the same innovative corporate mind-set that you started out with.

Beware of false destinations. Don't look back and congratulate yourself on how far you've come. Look forward and think about how far you have to go. When implementing a dream strategy, there are no rest stops. You have to keep moving, keep changing. The evolution has to be ongoing.

A little success can be a dream strategist's enemy. It can foster a false sense of security.

During our transition period, I believe many of Spiegel's employees were prey to that trap. We needed a catalyst, something tangible to rouse everyone out of their lethargy. Some significant action to demonstrate that greater things were possible. I was confident that sign would come. When it did, it came from a most unlikely source.

The $100 Dress

One of our buyers secured a beautiful cream-colored summer dress for a promotion. It cost $100, a price that was significantly above similar dresses featured in the catalog. Created by designer Jackie Rodgers, the dress was stylish and strikingly original. I wasn't sure that our customers were ready for a dress with such a high price point and such an unusual design. But I decided we should take a chance.

We pulled out all the stops in the catalog presentation, putting the dress on a gorgeous model and using a top fashion photographer. The page jumped out at the reader; it looked more like a spread in a classy fashion magazine than something from the Spiegel catalog.

Almost immediately, we sold two thousand dresses, far beyond our expectations. It went like a ripple through the industry. An article in *Women's Wear Daily* recounted our triumph. Department stores jumped all over Jackie Rodgers, asking her how she dared sell to a catalog house. Jackie Rodgers, who was ecstatic about the sales, told the department stores that when they sold two thousand dresses she'd take their complaints more seriously.

Jackie Rodgers wasn't a top-level designer, and there were far more expensive and fashionable dresses in department stores. But we'd made our point. We proved that if you had the right item, if you photographed it exquisitely and created a certain level of fantasy, you could sell it through a catalog regardless of price.

The Jackie Rodgers dress reenergized the dream. From assistant buyers to vice presidents, everyone at Spiegel started thinking bigger and better. Hank really hasn't been talking through his hat, they said to one another. We really don't have any limits. Maybe, just maybe, we can ascend to a level above Jackie Rodgers. Perhaps we can approach the world's top designers without getting laughed out of their offices.

In the following months, we decided to find out.

CHAPTER EIGHT

From Europe's Runways to Spiegel's Pages

After our success with the Jackie Rodgers dress, anything seemed possible. Around the office, people started dropping names of top designers: Liz Claiborne, Giorgio Armani, Perry Ellis. Those names were magic. If we could fill our catalog with designer name fashions, it would mean more than increased profits. A great deal more.

It would show the world that Spiegel had arrived.

We were at the point in our dream strategy where we needed a push to get over the top. Just a few more obstacles to overcome and we'd make it. I needed to generate the momentum to get us there. The last thing I wanted was for my people to look down— either to be scared by the possibility of falling or to find an overly secure niche and enjoy the false comfort.

I realized the quest for designers would generate the desired momentum. It then became a matter of finding the people and tactics to begin that quest.

The Designer-Hunters

In the early eighties, I brought two key people to Spiegel: Judy Daniels and Linda Lisco. Judy had a retail background, working for the Carson Pirie Scott department-store chain in Chicago. She had excellent contacts with quality fashion sources and a thorough knowledge of different lines of women's clothes. Linda was the fashion director of the Charles Stevens stores in Chicago. She had also run her own design business, providing a showcase for young local designers. More than anything else, Linda had a handle on the latest fashion trends.

Working with Spiegel VPs Leo Sansone and Walter Killough, Linda and Judy drew up a hit list of designers. They divided the list into three categories: better, bridge and designer. The better category included Liz Claiborne, Ellen Tracy, Carol Little— primarily mainstream American designers. The bridge group, such as Anne Klein II, were a bit more daring and expensive. The designer category was the trendiest, hottest level, primarily elite European designers such as Armani, Versace and Rizonni.

Judy and Linda took their first steps with the better category. They understood that the bridge and designer groups were out of our league, and they figured their best chance was with the mainstream category. Judy had a contact at Liz Claiborne from her time at Carson's, and she decided to wage an all-out campaign to get Liz on board.

We knew Liz Claiborne was a perfect fit for Spiegel. Her designs represented fashion newness without radical changes in shape or silhouette. It was classic fashion with a twist, and it allowed women to experiment with new colors and fabrics without feeling like they were going off the deep end. Her clothes would appeal to our growing base of professional women— women who were just starting to get their feet wet in the working world; women who were starting their first job as an account executive with an ad agency, a junior attorney with a law firm or as an auditor with an accounting firm. They didn't want anything outlandish, but they wanted something stylish and comfortable.

Liz Claiborne was just starting to take off when Judy made her first call. They weren't the powerhouse they would eventually become, but they had a recognizable, accepted name.

Judy gradually wore down their resistance. To assuage their doubts, she made a number of promises: we'd use models that reflected the "Liz look"; we wouldn't market any merchandise prematurely, so their retail clients wouldn't be offended; we'd offer the merchandise at the same prices as department stores (we wouldn't undercut them).

After a number of visits, they finally agreed to try us for one season, adding that if there were any problems—with their retail clients or anything else—they'd drop us immediately.

We didn't get their hottest fashions, nor did we get large quantities, but it was a coup nonetheless. When I joined Spiegel, it was inconceivable that our catalog—or any catalog, for that matter—would carry a designer like Liz Claiborne. Having Liz's fashions in our book was news. When those first designs sold well, it was even bigger news. Suddenly, the industry and the media began to notice us. What was going on at Spiegel?

The timing of acquiring Liz as a source was fortuitous. Liz Claiborne fashions were becoming "hot"; we reaped the benefits of having a trendy designer in our catalog. We also sold a huge amount of her merchandise, reaping sizeable profits. Judy went to other designers and name-dropped. Liz was a magic three-letter word, and soon we had commitments from others in the better category.

But it was only the start of a new phase for the company.

Setting the Stage for Fashion

We brought Linda Lisco to Spiegel shortly after Judy arrived to create a fashion department. Before Linda's arrival, fashion was only a vague concept at Spiegel. Linda's objective was to formalize that concept, to create a distinctive and unified fashion style for Spiegel, one that everyone within the company could understand and adhere to.

Linda set our fashion standards regarding designers, looks and trends. It wasn't enough to have scattered items throughout the catalog that fit our fashion definition; it wasn't enough to have a majority of fashionable merchandise if they represented disparate types of fashion.

We wanted to get our customers to look at us as purveyors of real style. We wanted them to believe that we were "in the know." Ideally, our customers would use us much as they used a fashion magazine—if it was shown on our pages, it was "in." If we could get to a point where our book would reflect what was happening on the streets of New York, Paris and Milan, then we'd be where we wanted to be.

Linda and Judy went out on the designer circuit, signing up better designers. Even after they signed up the first wave of designers, there were formidable barriers. Our designer sources had never worked with a catalog house, and they had to be educated about our business. The time frame was an especially thorny problem. We didn't have a retailer's luxury of purchasing a design and quickly putting it in the store. We needed to photograph our products months in advance of the catalog publication date. Consequently, we had to work with tight deadlines. In many instances, we chose what we wanted from sketches and swatches, trying to visualize what the actual product would look like. Also, some of the designers limited our choices, allowing us to choose from a second- or third-tier group of fashions. Despite these difficulties, we were getting quality names in the catalog— Ralph Lauren and Perry Ellis came on board shortly after Liz Claiborne.

Once we had a handful of American designers, Judy and Linda headed for the European fashion capitals. It was the first of a number of European tours. Their purpose was not only to bring back top designers, but to get a sense of what was happening and translate it into our catalog.

Initially, the top designers turned up their noses at an invitation to show their wares in a catalog; the Italian designers were especially difficult. But Judy and Linda did manage to convince some of the up-and-coming French designers to give us a chance with the promise that we would show their stuff just as it was shown on the runways of Europe; we'd use the same fashion photographers that the slick magazines used.

Those first European fashions featured in the catalog didn't generate many sales. They were too expensive for most of our customers and too radical in design. But we were more than compensated by the attention we garnered. *Women's Wear Daily* ran a story headlined, "Spiegel Goes Couture." Another publication ran an article titled, "Have You Seen a Spiegel Catalog Lately?"

The momentum was building. Not only were our sales and profits climbing, but we were on the leading edge of the biggest catalog boom the industry had ever experienced.

A Better Way of Shopping

By 1983, the number of catalogs and the volume of sales they produced had soared. The very factors that contributed to Spiegel's success—toll-free numbers; emerging, segmented markets; improved direct-marketing techniques; lifestyle changes—fueled the catalog boom. Catalog sales had become a $40 billion market.

Though all the old players were still the largest—Sears, Wards, Penneys and Spiegel—there were hundreds of newcomers with highly specialized books. One of the best was Roger Horchow's. Filled with unusual and upscale home merchandise, the Horchow catalog had been around since 1971. But it didn't really take off until the early eighties, and it was a sign of things to come. Sharper Image, Land's End, Eddie Bauer, L.L. Bean, Hammacher Schlemmer and many others implemented niche marketing approaches, zeroing in on their own special group of consumers and making it their own.

The competition was terrific for Spiegel. If we had lost some customers to the competition, we more than made up for it with an influx of new customers. We were the beneficiaries not only of our own efforts, but the industry's. Suddenly, shopping by catalog was not only acceptable, it was trendy. It was a time-saving alternative. It was a mode of shopping that appealed to a more affluent group than ever before.

Spiegel was riding the crest of the catalog wave. As the pioneer in this new type of catalog, we had a tremendous advantage over our competitors. While they were just starting to define their markets, create their databases and launch their books, we had done all that and more years earlier. Everything we'd labored to build was right on the mark. In the race to capture this market, we had a head start.

All dream strategies require a certain amount of anticipation. Although no one can predict the future, you can make some educated guesses. From the very beginning, I guessed that the ranks of career women would swell. I suspected that they'd be receptive to an alternative to traditional shopping. I assumed that the toll free number and database marketing would transform the catalog business, loosening the big three's stranglehold on the catalog business. I had a hunch that if we created a Spiegel culture that was flexible and in a state of constant change, we'd be prepared to take advantage of coming trends.

Not all of my guesses were correct. But enough of them were, and Spiegel was sitting pretty. Like a chess player, we were planning our moves far in advance, conceptualizing how the board would look twenty or thirty moves later. We had placed our company in the perfect position.

The Elite

Castelbajac, Catherine Hipp, Azzedine Alaia, Kansai Yamamoto, Ardi, Ann Marie Berette. Those were the premier designers, the crème de la crème. Their names were synonymous with haute couture.

We got all of them.

Each top designer acquired was a triumph, a culmination of many visits and haggling over conditions. But it was inevitable. With hindsight, it appears obvious that all the designers were lined up like dominos. Once we got the first few, the others fell in line.

We offered something that was impossible to resist: a national market of fashion-conscious women and a high-class vehicle created to reach them. Not incidentally, we also offered designers the chance to make significant profits.

In fact, we began to have trouble keeping up with the demand. It wasn't just our sources who had to learn how to work with us. We had to learn how to work with them. In more than one instance, we woefully underestimated the demand for an item. We anticipated five hundred orders for a dress and instead got a thousand. We couldn't simply reorder from the source and expect the dresses to arrive the next day. Many times, they were out of those dresses, and new fabric had to be ordered and cut.

Gradually, however, we began to develop bonds with our new suppliers. It helped that we were becoming invaluable to Liz Claiborne, selling millions of dollars of her label annually. The top designers cast envious eyes at our success with Liz, and they were willing to change their policies to meet our requirements. They began giving our people ''sneak previews'' of designs for coming seasons; we saw them before the department store buyers. It wasn't too long before people grabbed our catalog to learn what the next hot fashion trend would look like.

Norma Kamali

The nature of fashion in America was changing. No longer were the top designers relegated to an isolated perch far removed from the masses. Television, especially, was having a profound impact on the ''democratization'' of fashion. You didn't have to be in the business to know who Anne Klein, Liz Claiborne or

Yves St. Laurent were. All you had to do was watch prime-time television and you'd see a commercial for one of those designers.

No longer did fashion start on the coasts and slowly move toward the center of the nation, taking months or even years until a new fashion concept took hold. The pace of fashion accelerated. You could see a fashion show from Paris on cable television and instantly be aware of new design trends.

All of this gave Spiegel the necessary impetus to move our dream in new directions. We had to keep reaching for the next rung on our strategy. Now that we had the designers, we had to merchandise them creatively. We had to demonstrate clearly— both to ourselves and to the outside world—that Spiegel's dream was flexible and innovative; that it didn't have an endpoint.

The idea of a specialty catalog wasn't new anymore. The idea of a specialty catalog devoted exclusively to the fashions of one designer was. Norma Kamali wasn't just any designer. She was the epitome of high-fashion, the New York designer who had created the layered look. Her style had a name—OMO (on my own)—and it was sexy, stylish and daring.

We not only convinced her to let us devote an entire catalog to her designs, but also to create designs exclusively for that catalog. The resulting forty-page catalog featured everything from swimsuits to couture, ranging in price from $10 to $7,000. Though we didn't sell many of the $7,000 gold lamé evening dress she created, it was the talk of the industry.

We used top New York photographers to capture the Kamali look, creating a catalog that some magazine writers compared to *Vogue*. We mailed it to 500,000 Spiegel customers, and it wasn't long before the orders poured in. Our Kamali collection was the subject of scores of articles, many of them praising the catalog and expressing shock that Spiegel was the one to do it.

The Kamali catalog, more than any other single designer we had secured, showed the world we were serious about what we aspired to be. All traces of the old Spiegel were scattered to the winds when the Kamali book was launched. No one could doubt our commitment. We were putting our money where our mouth was: the Kamali catalog represented a huge monetary investment. It was a symbol of how far we had come and the direction we wanted to go.

The Spiegel Strike Force

I opened this chapter by talking about Judy Daniels and Linda Lisco and their contributions to Spiegel's strategy. There were many other key people, including vice presidents Walter Killough, Leo Sansone and Marian Larson. Without those five and the others who worked with them, we couldn't have convinced one designer to consider letting us display his or her wares.

A dream strategy depends on a special type of person. The five individuals I just mentioned were different ages and had different personalities, but all of them had one essential thing in common: they were at the peak of their careers, ready to try something big and risky.

When recruiting new employees and deciding which ones I wanted to keep, I had looked for energy, imagination, ambition, drive. I also knew what I didn't want: game-players, plodders, those biding their time until retirement, bureaucrats.

By 1981, I had the people I wanted in place. In the early eighties, they led the hunt for the top designers. Each manager shared my sense of vision; each one was inspired by the dream of a fine department store in print. Their energy was inexhaustible. In their quest for top designers, they refused to take no for an answer. I could give them direction—I could say, get me Kamali—but they were the ones who had to do it.

Every dream strategist should search for employees who have the capacity to dream and the desire to bring the dream to life. Don't delude yourself. No matter how glorious your vision, you can't do it alone.

CHAPTER NINE

Transforming Perceptions

No question, the changes we made in Spiegel's apparel lines were critical. But if we had only worried about stocking the catalog with designer names, we would have overlooked a major part of the dream strategy.

We had to change everything! We couldn't have a cheap, ugly bedspread in the same catalog with a $1,000 evening gown. Everything from draperies to clocks to beds had to undergo the same transformation as our apparel merchandise. We needed to continue to upgrade our home furnishings sources, creating a uniform sense of fashion throughout the catalog. But we had another, more ambitious goal.

We were acutely aware of the emerging role of life-styles in purchasing decisions. You could no longer lump all working women above a certain income in the same category. All categories were splintering along life-style lines. There were those people who had an outdoor life-style; a casually elegant life-style; a conservative, traditional life-style.

We needed to target our marketing to those segments. Luckily, the dream strategy was sufficiently flexible to accommodate this change. My idea was to create catalog pages that moved away from the typical department store display—a page of chairs, a page of sofas, a page of linens—toward a presentation of life-style.

Again, this new direction wasn't easy for everyone to accept. I was going to be asking everybody in the company once again to alter their thinking about our catalog.

But we had to do it. Every dream strategist has to anticipate and react to marketplace changes. You've got to be fast on your feet. In fact, as a dream strategist, you have to be faster than everyone else.

Rather than looking at this latest wrinkle in our plan as a problem, I saw it as an opportunity. I didn't worry about all the changes we'd have to make and whether we could make them. Instead, I got everyone at Spiegel excited about life-style marketing. "This is terrific," I told them. "We're going to be the first catalog that takes advantage of it. Let's do it fast and let's do it right."

Total Look Pages

Working with my vice president, Al Paul, we devised our tactics. The essence was a catalog page that would be unlike anything we or anyone else had ever done. It would be a page populated by a diverse group of merchandise tied together by a life-style.

Catalogs, Spiegel's included, had always had a product focus. You might have a bedroom scene with different objects, but the page's objective was to sell the bed. The other items were props. And usually the props looked insignificant; you didn't want to detract from the featured item.

Our concept of total look pages was the opposite of this approach. We wouldn't just sell the bed; we'd sell the picture behind it, the vase on the nightstand, the rug in the foreground, the pillows, the linens, the blankets, the chair to the side and the blinds covering the window. Each product would reflect a life-style theme. Perhaps one page would appeal to the affluent, single woman whose life was her career. Another page would target the married, suburban couple. No matter what the life-style, however, all the merchandise would be highly fashion-conscious, similar to our philosophy toward apparel.

It wasn't easy for the buyers to adapt to this new concept. In one sense, this was an even more radical departure than our move from utilitarian to fashion-conscious merchandise. The selection process we proposed was unlike anything they had ever experienced.

In the past, for instance, buyers would choose a lamp they thought appropriate for the lamp page. Now, they had other factors to consider. Let's say the page was geared toward an outdoor life-style. The spread under discussion was a patio scene. During the planning conference, the buyer couldn't fix on one deck chair she wanted to plant on the page. Depending on the life-style targeted, her favored deck chair might be totally inappropriate. It might not fit with the patio table. Or it might not work with the overall theme of the scene.

We instructed buyers to come to planning meetings with a number of alternatives for each piece of merchandise on a page. Instead of one choice for a deck chair, they had to have seven, maybe even more. That meant a lot of hard work and contacts with numerous sources.

It also meant they had to understand different life-styles. We educated them. Our stylists conducted many life-style conferences for the buyers and advertising people, explaining what caused certain items to appeal to certain groups.

No longer could the buyer say: "I want that carpet to go there." The role of the page stylist now became critical, picking and choosing among hundreds of items to achieve the proper effect. We positioned items on a page in order of importance. We'd decide that a certain item would receive the primary focus, another would get the secondary focus and so on. Working with photographers, we carefully lit a set to achieve the desired impact.

It took us years to get everyone on the right wavelength, but when they were, we were rewarded for our efforts. Spiegel's policy became: If we show it, we sell it.

Making Trends Happen

Our total look pages had a tremendous impact. Not only were they the envy of the industry, but they tremendously increased our sales and set off chain reactions in the marketplace.

For instance, we decided to devote one total look page to an old-fashioned type of bed. We were able to obtain a large quantity of beds at an attractive price from one of our sources. The page looked terrific and the sales were terrific. Shortly thereafter, our old-fashioned brass beds were one of the hottest products in the home furnishings industry.

Our success with brass beds wasn't an isolated event. We found ourselves in the enviable position of being able to suggest what was fashionable. Our total look pages, high-quality merchandise, and our increasingly large and loyal customer base enabled us to set trends rather than follow them.

We had the Midas touch—the majority of merchandise we featured turned to profits. Customers were regularly making multiple purchases, hooked by the total look pages. They weren't only buying one item on a page; it was only natural that they'd want the accompanying items, feeling that everything went so well together. There were even times when people bought everything on the page!

Sears, Wards and Penneys tried to copy us, but they simply couldn't do what we had done. Those organizations were not built for rapid change. They weren't corporate dreamers. Try as they might, they didn't have the flexibility to redesign their books radically.

By 1984, we had carved out our niche. No one could touch us. We were well on our way to becoming a billion dollar company.

Winning the Media

The media, more than any other group, was skeptical about our dream. Despite some of the favorable publicity we had generated, we recognized that a sizeable number of reporters and editors still weren't convinced we were for real.

By the nature of their jobs, fashion reporters are sophisticated and skeptical. They're innundated with press releases filled with hype about the next fashion trend, the hottest new designs. They rub shoulders with the top designers and marketing people from the big chains and companies. As a result, they take everything with a grain of salt, and it takes a lot to impress them.

We needed the media on our side. If the most influential magazines and writers wrote favorable articles about what we were doing, it would be the ultimate affirmation. Once *House Beautiful, Vogue* and *Women's Wear Daily* anoint you a fashion leader, there's no room left for doubt.

Along with our public relations agency, Burson Marsteller, we'd been using all the traditional public relations tactics: press kits, releases, backgrounders, one-on-one interviews. But we needed something more. Something that would be sufficiently attention-getting and out-of-the-ordinary, something that would communicate our dream had come to pass.

We created unusual and entertaining events at pleasant meeting places and resorts, making it easy for our friends in the media to attend. We had an important retailing innovation to sell, an innovation that in our opinion was very newsworthy.

The Spiegel story was becoming big news around the industry and the media accepted our invitations not only to have a few days of fun and relaxation, but also to have the opportunity to mingle with top designers and major fashion producers, as well as with Spiegel executives. This communication vehicle helped us get our big message across—that Spiegel was creating a national department store in print, that we were providing a better way of shopping for millions of busy American women who had little time to shop in stores.

CHAPTER TEN

Breaking All the Rules

You can't create a dream strategy that's a variation on a theme. It has to be new. You've got to come at customers from a different angle with an original pitch.

For eight years at Spiegel, we did everything backwards, sideways and against the grain. We ignored tradition. We did things no one else had done before. We sold to a market that didn't exist or hadn't been defined when we started.

We broke all the rules.

We didn't break them for the fun of it. It's just that if you're a nontraditional company, you have to do things in nontraditional ways. If we had tried to market our catalog like Sears or relied on standard mail-order concepts, we would have failed.

Let's look at some key rule-breakers of a dream strategist.

Rule-Break 1: Identify the Customer Before the Product

IBM produces a new computer and then creates a marketing program to sell it to a targeted customer base. General Foods comes up with a great new idea for a frozen dessert and then searches for an audience to sell it to. General Motors comes up with an expensive sportscar and searches for a market segment that will buy it.

I'm not implying that these companies don't conduct focus groups and research the market. I am saying that, in most instances, product takes precedence over customer. Many corporations operate under the "better mousetrap" theory. They assume that, given superior products, the world will beat a path to their doors.

All very logical. At Spiegel, we did the opposite, working from the outside in.

Long before we had the type of catalog we wanted, we defined and targeted the customer. We were still selling a bargain-basement catalog while we dreamed about a department store audience.

From a traditional marketing perspective, we were doing things backwards. It's all well and good to have a great marketing concept, but if you don't have the product to back it up, you're selling smoke. Here we were, a second-rate catalog house on the verge of bankruptcy, planning on selling to a nonexistent market of affluent working women who we believed were looking for a better way to shop. We were spending countless hours profiling this market even though we didn't have the merchandise, catalog or services that would appeal to it.

Why? Because if we correctly anticipated the emergence of this new group of consumers, we'd be one step ahead of the game. Form would follow function. Once we had our customer squarely in our sights, we could design our fine store in print to meet her needs. When she emerged, we'd be there ready and waiting with the product.

If we had tried to do it the other way around—creating our ideal catalog before fully defining the customer—we would have missed the mark. We would have created a catalog that wouldn't have captured the imagination of working women. We would have been forced to shoehorn the catalog into the market, and it wouldn't have been a good fit.

Everything we did flowed from the customer. A lot of companies talk about being customer-driven. But in many cases, that's all it is: talk. Our dream of a new customer shaped our product.

Rule-Break 2: Don't Wait for the Trends
to Come to You

How many companies market toward existing trends? Too many. They're poised to jump on whatever comes into vogue. When a fitness craze hits, companies rush to come out with products that cater to that obsession. When the headlines declare that certain types of food have disease-fighting capabilities, companies market new and existing products in that direction.

The problem, of course, is that few companies are quick enough to jump on the trends. Or the competition is too thick. If you have sufficient marketing muscle and dollars—and a truly beneficial product or service—perhaps you can take advantage of a trend while it's happening. Most likely, though, you'll be too late.

Another approach is to create a product or service in anticipation of trends. No one has a crystal ball. No one can say with certainty what's going to happen a year or five years from now. But you can make assumptions. Educated guesses. Research-informed suppositions. Projections. Visions and dreams.

At Spiegel, we did all of that and more. We created a catalog for the future rather than the present.

We believed that a new upper-middle class was being created. Prior to 1976, the middle class was primarily made up of one-income families. But the middle class exploded with the rise of two-income households, the increase in wages secured by equal opportunity laws and numerous other factors. Suddenly (or so it seemed) there were countless couples with combined incomes over $40,000. They had sufficient disposable income to be ideal Spiegel customers. As more and more people joined the new two-income middle class, more and more of them became Spiegel customers.

We suspected that Americans would continue to develop more discerning and more specialized tastes. In the past, immigrants and the children of immigrants had far more immediate concerns (like putting bread on the table) to be discriminating shoppers. Most people of my generation didn't agonize over the color of kitchen appliances. But younger people with time and money began to shop selectively. Colors, shapes and materials all took on greater importance. Matters of taste created mini-trends such as home cooking, outdoor living, the European look. Quality and value became more important than price.

Spiegel was perfectly positioned to take advantage of these trends. We were the first catalog house to recognize that chrome wasn't the answer to every appliance, to target emerging life-style groups, to be there with trendy merchandise when the trends started.

For example, we targeted the outdoor market. When I was growing up, only rich people had patios. By the eighties, not only were patios part of the mainstream, but so too were decks, pools, and landscaped gardens. Before anyone else realized what was happening, we were devoting page after page to lawn chairs, patio tables, barbeque accessories. And our catalogs were already being sent to the people who were turning outdoor living into a major trend.

Other trends came to pass, such as the direct marketing revolution, toll-free ordering, home shopping. Unlike other companies, Spiegel was built to capitalize on these trends. As I've already pointed out, Spiegel was flexible. I wanted us to be able to change direction quickly if the situation called for it. I was not building another Sears or Wards. I was constructing a company that was intensely responsive to changing customer tastes and attitudes.

Why aren't all companies like this? Because there's risk. Companies like sure things. Boards of directors understand designing a strategy that capitalizes on current trends. They don't understand strategies geared for trends that haven't yet happened. At Spiegel, the biggest risk was that the working woman I visualized wouldn't emerge; or if she did, she wouldn't have the purchasing power or exist in the numbers necessary to make Spiegel profitable.

But corporate dreamers have to trust their instincts. As much risk as there was, I never doubted my vision. If I had, that doubt would have spread throughout the organization, and we would never have achieved what we did.

Rule-Break 3: Rise Above the Category

Every company is in a category. You're a credit card company, a food manufacturer, a franchise operation, a high-tech organization.

Too often, companies become slaves to their categories. They follow industry practices; they adhere to industry traditions; they become overly concerned with their competition's actions.

As a corporate dreamer, you have to rise above all that. You have to remake the category in your own image.

As a catalog company, we were lumped into the mail order group, but we needed to transcend that category. Even if we became an excellent mail order company, we'd be limited by our designation. We'd be stereotyped as a direct marketer, and there were many potential Spiegel customers who'd never buy anything from a mail order house.

A great many people lack confidence in the mail order process. If they had a bad experience ordering something by mail—which is not that uncommon—they'd be reluctant to shop by mail a second time. This was a special problem for the mail order category, and we had to overcome it. We decided to make Spiegel into a company that would be judged independently of the process.

We did so with a series of innovations, starting with the implementation of toll-free ordering. We also worked out an arrangement with UPS to speed the delivery and pickup of merchandise, virtually eliminating long delays between ordering and receiving products.

Another important innovation was a no-questions-asked return policy. We clearly communicated to our customers that if they were dissatisfied with a purchase, all they had to do was call us and we'd pick it up and credit their account. Even though we recognized this was going to boost our return rate, it was a critical step in our category-busting plan. We realized that many people are wary of ordering from catalogs because they're buying something without actually seeing, touching or trying on the product. They worry about what will happen if the product doesn't fit or if they don't like the color. With our guarantee of easy returns, we did away with that worry.

We also moved away from traditional mail order policies concerning credit. In the past, catalog companies like Spiegel hounded customers who didn't pay on time, hiring collection agencies to harass customers and even taking title when there were delinquencies.

We wanted Spiegel to make a greater effort to predetermine credit worthiness, thus accepting a more limited market size but better credit quality. Despite the dire warnings we received from financial people, we adhered to that policy without exception. Amazingly, in the eight years that we had this policy, our bad debts went down from 7 percent to 3 percent. Of course, that decrease was due in part to our targeting of more affluent customers. But it was also a result of a bond of trust we were building with our market. We were telling them: We'll be good to you if you're good to us.

If a customer wanted credit, we didn't subject her to an unending series of questions about her credit history. Instead, we created a short form that was friendly and nonintrusive. Ideally, we wanted her to perceive Spiegel credit as cash-flow management, similar to a credit card. We didn't want customers who used credit because it was the only way they could afford a purchase.

It wasn't only the mail order category that we had to rise above; it was also the catalog category. One of the ways we separated ourselves from other catalogs was through our magazine advertising. We avoided the typical catalog ad media, such as *People* and *TV Guide* (magazines recommended to us by our first agency). Instead, we focused on more sharply targeted publications with better educated, more affluent readers—magazines like *Vogue* and *Better Homes*.

The ads we ran were also atypical. We disdained the ''preview'' approach—showing a selection of catalog items advertised at sale prices. Our ads were image-oriented. They sold readers on a new, better way of shopping. When we featured a product, it was a well-known, designer name.

All our ads featured a response card offering a catalog to readers. What shocked many people—both customers and the catalog industry—was that the catalog wasn't free. We were charging $3.00. That was unheard of at the time, violating all the precepts of catalog marketing.

We weren't trying to make a profit on catalog sales; it cost us more than $3.00 to produce each catalog. We had a more strategic motive: to raise the perceived value of our book. People judge things by what they pay for them. If something costs nothing, it's worth nothing. The Spiegel catalog was something of value. If you wanted to shop in our catalog, you had to pay for the privilege.

Certainly more people would have responded to our catalog offer if it had been free. But they would have been the wrong type of people. We had no desire to snare typical catalog buyers. We were creating a new category, and we wanted a new category of catalog customers.

Rule-Break 4: Don't Put the Squeeze On for Profits

Numbers-crunchers are death to dreams. If one eye is on the dream and the other on profits, you'll be hopelessly torn between the two.

103

At Spiegel, I never placed profits above all else. That might seem strange, especially in light of the current obsession with the bottom line and quarterly earnings. But a corporate dream is a fragile thing. It grows through a shared vision, through belief in a grand idea. When you let profits shape that idea—when you say, we can't do this because it's not profitable, even though it's the right thing to do—then you diminish the dream.

Don't get me wrong. I wasn't a pure idealist unconcerned about making money. It was just that I knew profits would follow the dream as surely as day follows night. The record $30 million in profits we were making when I left Spiegel is sufficient proof of that theory.

In 1984 we put in an elaborate, high-tech operating system for $22 million. At first, it was a catastrophe. Merchandise was lost in the warehouse, the computer misplaced inventory, and everything that could go wrong did go wrong. Even though sales were excellent, the operating system's implementation caused profits to plummet to $9 million.

But I never regretted the decision. The operating system was essential to the dream. Once all the bugs were eliminated, it would allow us to serve our customers better than ever before. If I had worried about the impact of the system on our profit-and-loss statement, I would never have purchased it.

My goal, however, was to build Spiegel into an institution, not a short-term moneymaking machine.

Throughout my tenure at Spiegel, I refused to seize every opportunity for increased profits. I refrained from marking up prices as high as we could have. I avoided bullying our sources into giving us better deals than the already good ones we had.

Spiegel's relationships with customers and sources were the best in the business. There was a foundation of trust and respect.

Even if we could have boosted profits by 20 percent, it wouldn't have been worth sacrificing that trust and respect.

Rules Are Made to Be Broken

When a child is told to be home by dark, why does he obey? Because he knows if he breaks the rule, he'll be punished.

But what if he breaks the rule for a good reason? He stays out late to help a younger child find her way home, or spends an extra hour practicing his jump shot because he dreams of being a good basketball player.

If the reason is good enough, he might escape punishment. He might even be rewarded.

Corporate dreamers have excellent reasons for breaking the rules. At Spiegel, we had no choice but to violate numerous management and marketing principles. It was our only way to escape our unattractive niche.

There was the possibility of punishment, I suppose. We could have gone bankrupt. But with each rule we broke, the possibility of punishment grew more remote. Every time we tempted fate and survived, we grew stronger. We grew more confident.

Gradually, we realized something wonderful, something every successful corporate dreamer finds: the more old rules you break, the more new rules you make. But they're your rules, no one else's.

CHAPTER ELEVEN

Growing Pains

Success has a price. As the corporate dream becomes reality—as things dramatically change—you have to adjust. You can't operate the company five years down the road the same way you did at the start.

Everything must change. Your marketing, management, operations—all must evolve. A growing company is very much like a growing person. You're not the same person at eleven as you are at twenty-five. An adult who continues to act like a child will run into difficulties. As one goal after another is achieved, you have to reorient yourself. There have to be shifts in the way you do business.

There are going to be growing pains. That's fine. You have to accept and deal with them. The best way of doing so is to put a monitoring system in place that will tell you where you've been and where you're going.

Vital Signs

Most corporations measure themselves financially. They have categories such as profits, revenues, return on investment.

Certainly we kept track of those things, but that's not the way I wanted to measure our progress. Most corporate employees outside of the financial area can't make heads or tails of arcane accounting terminology. They cannot relate to a 5 percent increase in return on investment. I wanted something everyone could understand and relate to.

I created Spiegel's Vital Signs. What are vital signs? You wake up in the morning and tell your mother you don't feel good and can't go to school. She puts her hand on your head and says, "Hank, go to school. You don't have a fever." That's a vital sign. Or the doctor uses his diagnostic equipment to determine how your heart is working and says, "It's ticking like a Swiss clock." That's another vital sign.

A company, like a person, has vital signs. Those signs are far more than numbers. In a turnaround situation, it's a mistake to put numbers to what you're doing. For instance: we have to achieve a 10 percent increase in sales by year's end. If you create these numerical goals, the dream starts to lose flexibility and everything becomes driven by financial success, budgets, requirements. You start making decisions based on the bottom line. You project that you'll make $5 million in the next quarter, and so you decide to cut staff and put on a hiring freeze, even though those actions are counterproductive to the dream.

We created charts which documented our vital signs. There were charts for sales, returns, merchandise turnover, mark-up, average inventory, number of active customers and much more. Each department had its own set of vital signs.

We tracked those signs over time. As long as the signs that should go up went up and the signs that should go down went down, we were satisfied. We didn't care about the percentage increase or decrease, as long as they went in the right direction.

For instance, when we mailed our first Discover Spiegel catalog, we started out with a 1.2 percent response rate. Every time we sent it, the percentage increased slightly. Eventually, it went up to 4 percent. But we didn't care about the specific increase. The fact that it was going up was sufficient. By watching that sign, everyone could chart our progress. It was simple and universally understandable.

We refused to attach numerical goals to those signs, demanding, for example, a 2 percent response from Discover Spiegel in two years. Of course, we didn't have forever; our owners wouldn't have tolerated that. So we allowed ourselves five years. To me, that was a reasonable time frame. Corporate dreams need reasonable time frames. Without them, you'll try to run faster than your feet can carry you. You'll be exhausted before the finish line is in sight.

Vital Signs served many purposes, but one of the most crucial was involvement. No one was in the dark about what was taking place at Spiegel. All our people could follow and chart the action as easily as someone at a baseball game with a scorecard. If there was a problem with one vital sign, a cover-up wasn't possible. We had to acknowledge the problem and take steps to return the sign to health. If a vital sign was good, everyone responsible felt confident.

Sharing the Wealth

Whenever a company achieves success—especially in a turn-around situation—there is the expectation of rewards. There's a danger to that expectation. If you single out certain individuals and reward them far beyond what you give others, you will encourage jealousy and resentment. If that jealousy and resentment is allowed to fester, it will undermine everything you've achieved.

Too often, companies give sizeable bonuses to reward individual performance. When I arrived at Spiegel, they had a bonus system in place that rewarded employees for fulfilling objectives. I did away with the old bonus system. First, I didn't believe in management by objectives, especially when geared to department objectives. The problem is that department objectives often are at odds with company objectives. The operations department's objective is to speed up the order-fulfilling process; one way they can achieve that goal is through a smaller average order. However, the company's larger objective is to increase average order size.

I instituted what I called the "World Series" approach to bonuses. If your team wins the World Series, even if you sat on the bench through the series, you share in the bonus that comes with winning. The theory is that you are part of the team, that you helped get them there.

Everyone who "got Spiegel there" received sizeable bonuses. Not just top managers, but anyone who had daily decision-making responsibilities, such as buyers. Individual performance had nothing to do with the size of the bonus. The factors we included in determining bonus amounts were management level (corporate officers received up to 40 percent of their base salary, the next level 35 percent and so on) and corporate profits after taxes.

It was a fair system that was almost universally applauded. If the company did well in a given year, so did the majority of employees.

Our owners didn't think much of my system. They believed in management by objectives and they thought personal performance should enter into bonuses. I vigorously defended my approach to the owners, explaining that their approach leads to brown-nosing and playing favorites. It also places an unfair emphasis on evaluations. Like teachers, some bosses are hard graders, others are easy graders. Employees understand this. Naturally, those with hard graders will resent a bonus system tied to performance evaluations.

The World Series bonuses inspired teamwork. They provided an incentive to work for the common good rather than individual goals. Of course, individual performance was rewarded. But it was rewarded through salary increases, not bonuses.

Crises

Crises are inevitable. You're sailing along through smooth seas when all of a sudden an angry cloud appears on the horizon. You watch it spread across the sky, advancing toward you. It

110

seems to have come out of nowhere. All you can do is watch it approach and wait for it to break. There's nothing you can do but prepare yourself to weather the storm.

In 1983, everything was going our way. Our record-making profit of $25 million was just the start of what seemed a string of record-breaking years. Nothing could stop the Spiegel dream.

Because of our rapidly escalating sales, we needed a new order-processing system. Our old system was woefully out of date, and we had to automate the process. We had seen how efficiently the computerized system our German owners had worked, and we purchased that system.

It was a disaster. We had decided to close for a few days during the summer to facilitate installation of the new system. We recognized that, unlike a department store, a catalog couldn't close for remodeling; there's no way to stop orders from coming in. But we assumed that we'd be able to pick up the slack once the system was up and running.

That was a bad assumption. It took more than a few days to get it going. In fact, it took more than a year. During that time, we had chaos in the warehouse. One day the computer would lose five hundred men's shirts. The next day it would be two hundred beds. Shipments to customers were delayed, and then delayed again. We were playing a costly hide and seek game with our merchandise.

From record profits of $25 million, we dropped the next year to barely breaking even. Sales were still climbing, but the new ordering system was taking money away from us as fast as we could bring it in.

During that terrible year, I tried to hold the company together. In a crisis, you need calm at the top. Everyone takes his or her lead from the CEO. If I panicked, they'd panic. Just as important, I didn't want to lose the closeness, the esprit de corps we had painstakingly built over time. When a crisis hits, finger-pointing is a natural, defensive reaction. I saw the early signs: merchandise people yelling at operating people that they weren't filling the orders, operating people countering that if they didn't have so many back orders, we wouldn't be in this mess.

I put an end to that quickly. I told everyone that I was taking responsibility, that no one else was to blame. I made it very clear that I didn't want to hear or see any backbiting. Though I couldn't eliminate the finger-pointing entirely, I think I effectively contained it. I prevented a technological crisis from destroying the human part of our business.

One way I did this was to point out that a new operating system was an absolute necessity. When everything is in shambles, it's hard to see the larger picture. But I explained why we needed a new system. More specifically, why our customers needed a new system. In the short term, it might have been easier to rely on our old, manual ordering process. But in the long run, the results would have been regrettable. Without a computerized system, we would never have been able to handle our growing orders; we would have failed in our goal of providing our customers with the best service possible.

So I counseled patience. I insisted that the crisis wouldn't sink us, that we'd muddle through until we worked the kinks out of the system. I didn't fire anyone because of the problems; I didn't turn anyone into a scapegoat. I kept on repeating: we'll get through this.

We did. Once the system was fully operative, our profits zoomed back up to the $25 million level and continued to rise in succeeding years.

Changing the Way You Do Business

Our relationships with "outsiders"—the media, sources, other suppliers—continued to evolve. It was inevitable. Any company that's growing at a rapid rate will repeatedly have to reevaluate how it deals with outside parties.

During my first few years at Spiegel, we approached new, quality sources far differently than our old sources. Our buyers had to adjust their approach, educating sources who had never worked with catalogs about our requirements. When they talked to buyers about keeping us supplied with merchandise, the sources said, "What are you talking about? This dress is going to be available for three months only, then we'll bring out a new item."

We finally figured out that the problem was with the fabric: they'd only ordered enough for three months' worth of dresses. So we made our sources an offer: we'd take partial financial responsibility for whatever fabric was left over if they ordered more fabric to fulfill our orders.

We also changed our strategy toward estimates. Typically, we'd provide our sources with estimated sales for a particular item. We'd estimate the high end and low end of sales and settle on a figure somewhere between the two. That would give the source a scale to determine how many items we'd need.

But with our new sources, we had no idea how many we could sell. We had no history with them. Our worst fear was that customer orders would exceed our supply of an item, and as a result we'd alienate customers, many of whom were making their first purchases from Spiegel.

We couldn't afford that. We decided to order more than 100 percent of our estimated sales. That way, we'd generally be able to fill most of our orders. The downside, of course, was when orders fell below expectations; we'd have to absorb the losses.

Our relationships with sources changed again as we became more successful. Once we proved to sources that we could sell a sizeable quantity of their merchandise, they were willing to make concessions to the needs of a catalog marketer. Suddenly, our buyers didn't have to beg. They could negotiate from strength for what they wanted.

No question, it was a difficult adjustment for buyers. It seemed that as soon as they become comfortable with one way of dealing with a source, circumstances changed and they had to take a new position. That they were able to adjust—and that we supported our buyers in the effort—contributed a great deal to our growth.

Integrity

Power corrupts, as does growth and success. The faster you grow, the more likely you'll be tempted to cut corners and take advantage of sources, employees and customers. Once you've achieved certain goals, there will be a tremendous amount of pressure to achieve even greater goals. Because of that pressure, it's tempting to adopt practices that are at best questionable and at worst unethical.

At Spiegel, I made it my business to communicate that none of these practices would be tolerated. I told the buyers that their word is their bond. I knew that they'd have situations where they'd run into problems with sources, and that the easiest solutions might involve deception. Time and again, I stressed that they were to ask sources for help if a problem occurred, that they were not allowed to sneak out of commitments.

At times, people would come up to me and say, "If we do this, we can save this." I'd ask them, "Is this fair?" And they'd respond, "Well, it's typical." I'd tell them, "I don't care about typical. I care about if it's the right thing to do."

I instilled fairness and ethical behavior into our culture. All employees were treated with consideration and concern. From salaries to bonuses to working conditions, I made every effort to make each employee feel rewarded and respected. As a result of this policy, we had no problems with the unions to which our employees belonged.

Too often, large, fast-growing companies have serious labor difficulties. They're caused by the employees' perceptions of an adversarial relationship between unions and employers, perceptions employers often foster. Our people were convinced that their long-term benefits were tied to Spiegel's success—as long as the company did well, so would they. I wanted each and every employee to be proud of being a Spiegel employee, as proud—or even more proud—as they were of their union membership.

We maintained the same integrity in our relationship with customers. Again, as you grow, it's easy to forget who brought you to the dance; to become subtly arrogant in your dealings with customers. To avoid that possibility, we took a number of actions. First, we established the position of customer advocate. The role of customer advocates was to respond to questions, concerns and complaints, taking the customer's side and trying to resolve matters so that customers would be satisfied. Even though they were employed by Spiegel, we told them that they were to safeguard the rights of our customers, not vested company interests.

We also handled customer complaints differently than most other companies. A typical mail order problem arose when something the customer ordered wasn't delivered. Rather than force the customer to prove that we were at fault—to sign documents, provide detailed descriptions of when they ordered the product, how they paid, etc.—we automatically assumed they were correct. At times, we even went overboard in trying to please our customers. More than once, a customer would receive two or even three of the same product because of our overzealous employees' desire to make them happy.

The CEO's Changing Role

When I first came to Spiegel, I did everything. Some people must have thought there was more than one Hank Johnson, since I seemed to show up everywhere—the mailroom, planning meetings, advertising conferences, display areas. After a while, I learned to concentrate on those tasks that only a CEO could perform, delegating responsibility to others.

A CEO running a growing company has to know how and when to make that shift. Once the major elements of the dream were in place—once everyone understood them and was carrying out his or her assignments—I had to move on to other things. Like developing a toll-free ordering system. Or participating in the strategy to capture Ralph Lauren as a source. They were longer-term objectives, and I was in the best position to help achieve them.

I stopped going to every planning meeting. I refrained from traveling with the buyers to every new market to meet every new source. As long as I was confident that my department heads were doing a good job, I turned to less immediate concerns.

Still, I kept a watchful eye over all departments and duties, providing my input if I thought someone was going off course.

Perhaps my most difficult adjustment was to the issue of succession. I had passed the company's retirement age, and our owners were pressing me to name a successor. I was reluctant to do so. I was excited about the many changes that were still taking place and didn't want to turn my dream over to someone else.

But I bowed to their request. I had brought Jack Shea in from Wanamakers, and he was my choice to continue building Spiegel. We underwent a transition period where I served as vice chairman and Jack became chief operating officer.

Jack has done a great job with Spiegel, helping them surpass the billion dollar mark in sales. He's running the company differently than I did, placing a far greater emphasis on profits. Perhaps that's appropriate. It's a different Spiegel now than when I was in charge, and maybe it's good that a new philosophy is in place.

As I've emphasized throughout this book, dreams aren't static. They have to be flexible; they have to evolve. A corporate dreamer has to be prepared to pass the baton to the next dreamer. As long as the core of the dream remains in place, a company will continue to grow and prosper.

CHAPTER TWELVE

The Perpetual Need for Change

It would be foolish to say that companies ignore change. Most are aware of what's happening around them and try to respond to events. But too often their focus is narrow and self-absorbed, and they're only responsive to certain types of change.

When a competitor introduces a new product, they react.

When a new technology is developed that will clearly influence their product category, they take steps to capitalize on that technology.

When their market share declines, they try to do things that will improve it.

There are other types of change. They are not always obvious, and their impact might be further down the road. When unheeded, change can devastate an organization, leaving managers scratching their heads and wondering where it came from.

Too often, companies are like sleepy yachtsmen, enjoying a beautiful day on the water. In the distance, a few clouds appear. More concerned about catching a fish, getting a good tan or reading the paper, no one pays any attention as the clouds gather and darken. If the yachtsmen happen to glance westward, they might acknowledge the potential for a sea change. But it's so far off and the sun is still shining. Why worry?

A few minutes later, the gathered clouds are roiling overhead, blotting out the sun. Soon, a monstrous storm breaks, the seas grow angry and toss the boat on huge waves.

Change can come quickly, seemingly out of nowhere. If you're not vigilant and poised to react, you'll be in danger.

Monitoring the Signals of Change

Changes are occurring at a faster pace than ever before. Environmental concerns, new modes of transportation and communication, foreign conflicts, economic problems—the list is endless.

Change filters down. When the environmental movement began, few corporations took much notice. They figured it would go away, like the 1960s protests against the military-industrial complex. Only it didn't go away. It picked up steam in the 1970s and 1980s, reaching a point where virtually every organization is affected by environmental concerns. Waste disposal, removal of dangerous materials in buildings, and pollution by smokestack industries are just some examples. "Biodegradable" wasn't a familiar word to corporate executives in years past. Now it's prominently displayed on countless product labels.

Change doesn't always translate easily to corporate strategy. A recent study shows that the nation's roads are falling apart, requiring billions of dollars of repair work. How will it affect a food products company? Or a cross-country trucking organization? Or an airline? It depends, obviously, on numerous factors, and it takes a leap of imagination to assess the impact.

You don't have to be a futurist to realize that life will be far different five or ten years from now than it is today. Take a simple test. Think back ten years. Think about words like frozen yogurt, triathlons, oat bran, antilock braking systems, wood decks, computer connectivity, aerobics, fax machines. It's hard to believe that merely ten years ago such words had little or no meaning. Today, they're part of our vocabulary. Consider all the changes that integrated them into our lives.

118

With hindsight, the forces of change are easily seen and understood. Of course, companies don't have the luxury of hindsight. In lieu of that, an acute awareness of what's happening in the world is essential. It means taking a long, hard look at the major forces of change, and assessing how they affect your organization.

You've got to be observant; otherwise you'll miss the signs of change. Change can be slow or fast. When it's fast, it's hard to miss. For instance, when Congress passes a new environmental protection law, companies suddenly have to conform to new standards.

Generally, however, change is slow and incremental. It's like a brand-new shower. At first, nothing seems to change. You take shower after shower and you don't notice anything different. But there are changes taking place. Hair and soap are building up in the drain; the chrome fixtures are losing their luster; the glass door is caked and streaky. It's only when the water starts backing up in the drain that you become aware that things have changed.

Those who are perceptive won't have to stand in a foot of dirty water before they take action.

Resistance to Change

Few companies would admit to being resistant to change. Yet many companies are. Why? A number of reasons.

First, their brains refuse to acknowledge the messages delivered by their eyes and ears. Look at the American automobile industry. The research capabilities of the Big Three automakers are enormous. Surely they must have received information that Americans wanted a smaller, more efficient, more economical car in the seventies. They were aware of the energy crisis and the declining sales of gas guzzlers. Despite all this, they allowed the Japanese to capture this new market with relatively inexpensive, reliable cars, the Americans lagging years behind in their efforts to capture this new market.

Second, change makes people uncomfortable. They realize change entails risk, disruption and hard work. Some organizations prefer to subscribe to the adage, if it ain't broke, don't fix it. It's an easier way of running a business. Of course, sooner or later, change results in breakage. The discomfort they encounter later will be far greater than if they had responded earlier.

Even minor changes make people uncomfortable. At Spiegel, our clerical staff was in an uproar when we changed from manual to computerized systems. They were terrified of switching from the familiar to the unfamiliar. Given the amount of resistance this minor change met with, you can imagine the increased resistance to far more sweeping changes.

Third, people in authority tend to be most resistant to change. Their authority may be threatened by change; they may be forced to give up some power or to shoulder greater responsibility. They may be forced to take risks. They might find that their staff of ten will be cut in half. A company only becomes responsive to change once top management accepts it as necessary and embraces new directions.

Fourth, vertically developed businesses are terribly resistant to change. A vertical company owns everything from soup to nuts, from manufacturing plants to distribution centers to materials suppliers. Because of this structure, they have a vested interest in maintaining the status quo. The prospect of revamping the entire system is intimidating. Vertical structuring should go the way of the cart and buggy. It is far better to own only a part of the network and contract with independent sources for the remainder. Such a structure makes it far easier to adapt to change.

Fifth, the bigger you are, the more resistant to change you're likely to be. There are a number of significant exceptions to this rule, but, by and large, size equals conservatism. It's simply the nature of the beast. Japanese car companies can create a new model in less than two years, while larger American auto manufacturers require five years. When larger catalog companies like Sears and Penneys saw Spiegel's success and tried to copy us, they failed. Their cultures couldn't accommodate the radical metamorphosis that was called for.

Refocusing

In the face of dramatic and sweeping changes, what can organizations do? How can they prepare themselves to react and take advantage of a changing world?

Let's take a small-scale example. A guy has a neighborhood jewelry store. For years he's made a good living, selling fine-quality merchandise, primarily engagement and wedding rings, to the middle-class residents of the neighborhood. In the last few years, sales have gradually declined. He still sells the same jewelry he's always sold. But the neighborhood has changed. The residents have aged, and senior citizens aren't interested in wedding and engagement rings. The new residents of the neighborhood have less disposable income, making his quality jewelry prohibitively expensive.

The jeweler is a victim of outside forces; he failed to assess his business from the outside in. His market changed and he didn't adapt.

What he should have done is refocus. He should have refocused his dream. With a new vision of his store, he might have been able to survive and prosper.

It's not easy. Not for a jewelry store owner and not for a Fortune 500 company. You have to fight inertia. You have to say to yourself: We've got to remake the business in a new image for a new customer.

Superficial changes are easy. Companies are always tinkering with advertising and distribution methods, shuffling personnel, creating new products and improving old ones. But I'm talking about far more dramatic changes here.

Consider the lawn-care market. For a long time, companies in that market did very well selling do-it-yourself products to homeowners—sprays, fertilizers, spreaders. Then someone realized that many homeowners were becoming too busy to take care of their lawns. They formed a company that you contracted to care for your lawn for an entire season. Suddenly, the do-it-yourself product companies were in trouble. They had ignored the trend that not only affected their industry but touched scores of other businesses, including Spiegel. People had less leisure time and were willing to pay for a service that saved them time.

Organizations have two options when faced with such change: either stubbornly stick with what they have been doing or find a new way.

For companies like Spiegel, that new way meant refocusing. More specifically, refocusing on a niche.

Niche marketing is such a logical response to rapid change that it's surprising more companies aren't doing it. The majority of organizations are still trying to be all things to all people. It's difficult to make an all-things approach work in an age of constantly changing market segments.

The ideal niche marketer won't be locked into one niche. They'll have the ability to move where their market is going, shifting their focus as dictated by emerging customer needs. The department store that specializes in home furnishings will shift its emphasis from kitchen to bedroom furnishings if the market moves in that direction.

Even the largest companies can adopt this approach. McDonald's, for instance, has done an outstanding job of refocusing over the years. They began as a fast-food establishment catering to families, a place to take the kids for a quick, inexpensive meal of hamburgers, fries and shakes. As things changed, they changed. They refocused on teenagers, on healthful alternatives to hamburgers (salads), on breakfasts for hurried working people.

McDonald's original dream—its vision of a clean, quality, fast-food restaurant—hasn't changed. But it's adapted to outside trends and events, reshaping itself to target niches right for them.

Embracing Change

What can companies do to make themselves more receptive to change?

They can begin by communicating their vision for the organization in a way that encourages people to look forward to change. If the CEO signals the company's new direction by saying, "Things are going to get tough around here for a while. We're going to have to tighten our belts, force ourselves to adapt to some new realities," then everyone will be uptight. Such a speech confirms their worst fears: change is unpleasant.

At Spiegel, I tried to communicate that change would be exciting, even exhilarating. Every day would be different. Every week would bring a new challenge. I guaranteed everybody that they wouldn't be bored. I promised that the coming years would be the most fun they'd ever had.

Those weren't just words. The vast majority of Spiegel employees *were* excited by the ride. They couldn't wait to see what was going to happen next.

How about predicting change? What can a company do to anticipate changes that seem far off but are quickly moving toward them?

Make forecasting the responsibility of top management. Don't look only at industry developments. Expand your horizons to the outside world. Perhaps a company creates a team of selected managers who examine all the signs for potential changes: newspapers and magazines, pending governmental bills, scientific studies, foreign conflicts, environmental issues. If the team recognizes a major change coming, they can immediately begin to deal with that change.

For instance, the team might notice a certain irony in American life: an increased number of families have two or more cars, but they are becoming more reluctant to travel to buy goods and services. They might come across a survey which shows 70 percent of Americans are dissatisfied with the speed at which services are delivered. They might be aware of the booming delivery business, how the majority of people are willing to pay a little bit extra to have products and services delivered to their homes or offices. They might have seen the rise of delivery pizza businesses and ten-minute oil-changes.

From all this, the team should conclude that Americans are busier than ever before, and are willing to pay higher prices if time can be saved. They can then analyze how this trend affects their business, and what changes they should make to capitalize on the trend.

The final thing a company can do to embrace change is very simple: remain open to new ideas. Very simple to say, very difficult to do.

People come up with all sorts of "good" reasons for not doing something new. "We tried that once and it didn't work." Or: "It sounds interesting, but let me play devil's advocate for a second." Or: "It's not in the budget." Or: "Our CEO hates that kind of thing."

Companies are great discarders of ideas. It takes a lot less time to say no than to say yes. When you say no, you don't have to invest time or energy in the idea. When you say yes, you're taking a risk; you've got to think about it, study it, put together a plan; you're putting yourself on the line.

For things to change, you've got to have an environment where new ideas flourish. An environment where even if the idea can't be used immediately, it's saved, nurtured, allowed to crystallize. When it's needed, it's there.

Strategies dictated by numbers, dictatorial CEOs, or rigid bureaucracies all are enemies of ideas. Create a company that's receptive to ideas and you'll create a company that's receptive to change.

CHAPTER THIRTEEN

Why Explain Why?

Supervisors and managers are very good at explaining what and how. The assembly line foreman can tell a worker exactly how to screw a bolt into a frame. The marketing director can clearly communicate to a brand manager what product should receive top priority in his advertising budget.

But when it comes to the why of things, they're hopelessly lost. Managers either don't have the skills to articulate the reasons for doing something or they aren't motivated to do so.

That's a serious flaw. If only the top few executives within an organization understand the why, their dream is in peril. Ultimately, the lack of company-wide knowledge about why they're doing what they're doing will catch up to them. The motivation for employees to add value—rather than maintain value—will be missing.

Without the Why

When I was at Aldens, there was a group of employees designated as control buyers. Their job was to keep tabs on merchandise in stock, projecting sales for a particular item and reordering from resources when the item ran short.

They didn't understand the why of their jobs. They carried out their tasks mechanically; they became nothing more than extensions of their computers. I remember once we had a product that was selling extremely well and I asked one of the control buyers about it.

"Yeah," he said, "number 4966 is a runaway."

"What's number 4966?" I asked.

"A blouse, I think," he said, uncertain because he was used to thinking of products as numbers.

"Who makes it?"

"I don't know."

"Why do you think it's a runaway?"

"I'm not sure."

"How is it presented in the catalog?"

"I really haven't looked at it."

The control buyers had been trained to think of themselves as clerks rather than merchants. They brought no enthusiasm, enjoyment or intelligence to their jobs. They had no incentive to speculate why an item was selling well or to suggest better methods of handling runaway orders.

I asked the control buyers' supervisor why this situation existed, and he said, "To go through explaining everything to each buyer would take too much time. If something's hot, I find out why, not them."

But why not them? Sure, it takes additional time. But it's time well spent.

At Spiegel, I made sure that everyone had a clear view of the bigger picture—top executives, middle-level managers, secretaries and clerks. The buyers understood why they were going after Source A rather than Source B. The order-takers understood why it was critical to communicate a certain image of the company in their conversations with customers.

Spiegel enjoyed a reputation as a great place to work, and that reputation was due in part to the corporate-wide understanding of the why. The vast majority of employees liked their jobs; each one of them felt they were performing a crucial function and that without them, Spiegel wouldn't run as well as it did.

The Generation Gap

More so than ever before, corporate employees want to understand the larger implications of their jobs. A far greater percentage of corporate workers have college degrees than in the past, and they also are better-trained and more sophisticated.

Invariably, there will be a clash between this group and the old guard—employees who rose through corporate ranks, starting in the mailroom (as I did) and working their way up.

My generation rarely learned the why. Our supervisors believed that it was not for us to reason why, only to do or die. We followed orders unquestioningly, and the corporate structure resembled the armed forces. Supervisors and managers were like grizzled drill sergeants, barking commands and keeping the troops in line.

Companies should pay special attention to the potential conflict between the two generations. Those entry-level college graduates (or even MBAs) are going to want to know why. To deprive them of that information is wrong; it will lead to higher turnover and lower morale. Old-guard supervisors and managers have to be trained to adjust to the new work force. They have to be willing to take the time to explain; they have to believe it's not a waste of time to do so.

The impetus has to come from the top. Organizations where only an elite group of top executives know what's going on can't provide it. They're so wrapped up in the "need to know" mentality that everyone else always feels left out.

Certainly there's a need for some secrecy; you don't want the competition to be prematurely aware of a new product or marketing plan. But in the majority of cases, an open and communicative management will have a trickle-down effect. Drill sergeant managers will soon follow the lead. They'll realize that the corporate philosophy encourages explanations, no matter who the employee is or what department he or she works in.

A Lesson from the Little Guys

If you put a small company and a big corporation on a level playing field, nine times out of ten the small group will win the race. They'll work faster, come up with better, more innovative ideas and implement them more effectively.

In most cases, small companies understand the reason why. Every employee knows what's going on. Each one understands not only his job, but how it relates to other people's jobs. They all have a vested interest in the success of the organization, and it's easy for them to translate what they do into how the company does.

There's a camaraderie that's energizing. When a new product is launched, everyone is rooting for its success.

It's difficult to maintain this culture as the company grows. You could make a long list of emerging growth companies that have lost their spark as they became larger.

The company brings in "outside" people to manage the growing business: a human resources manager from a Fortune 500 company, a financial wizard, a bunch of MBAs who have trained at a top consulting firm. These new people launch a variety of programs and policies that weren't needed when the company was small but are deemed appropriate for a larger organization. Clear-cut divisions of responsibility and knowledge emerge; the guy in operations no longer is able to put his two cents in about marketing. Soon, employees become estranged, complaining that "it's not like it used to be around here."

This isn't an inevitable process. Just because you're big doesn't mean you're destined to possess all the negative qualities of bigness. Big companies can maintain the same energy and spirit of little ones. They can make it their business to ensure that the why of things isn't limited to a select group of managers.

How to Keep the Why in the Open

There are countless ways to incorporate the why. I've touched on some of them already, and you'll find other suggestions in the remainder of this chapter.

I can't overemphasize that achieving the goal is only possible if an organization makes an unwavering commitment to provide the rationale behind what they ask their people to do.

That commitment can be demonstrated in many ways. One of the easiest is to eliminate the us-versus-them mentality. It's a mentality that shows up in discriminatory employee practices—practices such as unnecessary perks and exclusive arrangements for executive staff, including huge offices, segregated dining rooms, closed-door, hush-hush meetings.

As I've already explained, we didn't have any enclosed offices at Spiegel. Not for me or anyone else. That might seem like a small thing but it symbolized our philosophy. No hidden agendas. No cover-ups or misinformation. Everyone plugged into the network.

At many companies, the biggest worry is the quarterly profit-and-loss statement. My biggest worry was whether everyone understood our dream. What alarmed me more than anything else was an employee who was bored, who didn't bring any enthusiasm or ideas to his job. As soon as I or any of my managers saw an indication that this was the case, we labored to correct it. We focused our resources on converting every single Spiegel employee into a believer.

There wasn't anything mysterious or magical about it. It's something every organization can do. Give me an organization that grasps the dream—especially the why of it—and I'll give you an organization that can accomplish anything.

But while some companies may recognize the importance of the why, they inadvertently contribute to its demise.

One common mistake organizations make is to promote people for the wrong reasons. You're familiar with those reasons: "He's been here for years, it's time we moved him up"; "He really knows the business inside and out"; "She deserves the job. Nobody keeps the troops in line better than her"; "If we don't promote him, we'll lose him."

I'm not saying that seniority or superior business knowledge shouldn't be factors in promotions. What I am saying is that they shouldn't be the main criteria. When they are, the results are managers and supervisors who are merely competent. They're not the ones who can rally the troops around the corporate vision.

Communication skills should be a major factor in promotions. If a manager can communicate well, he or she has the ability to explain the why to subordinates. Of course, top management might have to motivate him to do so, but that's an achievable goal.

A good communicator can do more than simply explain. He can explain eloquently, motivationally, convincingly. He can raise the productivity level of each person he supervises, providing everyone with reasons to excel.

Arrogance and Secrecy

"When the reporter calls, tell him no comment."

"No one whose name isn't on the list is to see this document."

"It's only going to confuse our people if we explain why we have to cut staff by 10 percent."

It's easy to rationalize keeping people in the dark. To send terse press releases to the media that only hint at the company's true intentions. To limit employees' access to long-term plans on the assumption that they don't make major decisions. To paint a picture of the company for customers that is not an accurate reflection of the organization's guiding philosophy.

The why extends to employees, media, suppliers, customers, investment analysts—everyone. Don't keep your dream a secret.

130

Invite everyone to share it. The more people understand what you're doing the better.

When people believe in what you're doing, they're willing to extend their trust and loyalty. A company that communicates well and regularly with the media will generally receive more favorable coverage than a company that doesn't. A firm that has superior customer relationships will be forgiven more easily by customers when a mistake is made. A company that provides securities analysts with insights about their long-term objectives will be granted the benefit of the doubt when they have a bad quarter.

I received a dramatic lesson about the problems of arrogance and secrecy when I first arrived at Spiegel. I noticed that the company had suggestion boxes for employees to contribute ideas. I also noticed that the suggestions never were acted upon. When I discussed this incongruity with the supervisor in charge of the boxes, she said, "Oh, our people make the dumbest suggestions, you should see some of them. They ask us to do things that we can't afford to do or just don't make sense."

"Why do you think they do that?" I asked her.

"Because they don't have the faintest idea how things work around here."

"Maybe," I said, "if they knew how things worked, they'd make better suggestions."

She didn't get it, just as countless other managers don't get it. You can't automatically expect employees to add value to a company. The smartest, best-qualified employee is limited in what he can do if he feels excluded or demeaned.

Why Plus Freedom

You might be thinking that all this talk about the why sounds like the Japanese style of management. Yes and no. The Japanese system is great when it comes to encouraging each employee to think of himself as part of a whole. It certainly provides incen-

131

tives for corporate loyalty and innovation. No question, it gives precedence to the why.

But at what cost? At the cost of individualism. Each employee is a cog in the corporate machine, helping it run smoothly, efficiently and productively. The system demands that an individual fit his talent to the job.

I would much rather fit the job to the individual's talent.

American corporations have a long and honored tradition of encouraging employees to make the most of their singular talents. The best companies don't have rigid structures in place that demand conformity. The eccentric genius in research and development is given the freedom to work at his own pace using his own methods. The maverick marketing man is permitted to put his own, idiosyncratic stamp on the company's advertising.

Giving employees the why is not enough. They need the freedom to act on the why in their own unique ways, to improvise solutions rather than follow a script.

Spiegel accommodated as diverse a group of people—especially managers—as was possible. We had eccentrics, radicals, introverts and global thinkers. It was a wonderful mixture, and it ensured a wide range of ideas, approaches and solutions.

We would not have had that range if we subscribed to the Japanese style of management: everyone's movements perfectly synchronized by a master choreographer. I'm convinced a Japanese company could not have achieved what we did at Spiegel. They might have understood the dream, but they would have lacked the individual resources necessary to make it happen.

Bring the Why to Bear on Your Business

It's not just a people issue; it's a nuts and bolts business concern.

Organizations often fail to ask themselves the hard questions about their businesses. They don't probe or analyze their motives and goals; they don't dig below the surface to figure out what's really going on beneath the numbers.

They run their businesses by instinct and formula. This approach can work for a while. Good products and services, well-trained professionals, a receptive marketplace—all these things can carry a company for years. But they'll only take you so far. There are always obstacles down the road, and if you don't really understand the roots of your business, you can't clear them.

I know of a company that got off to a flying start, riding on the creativity of its founders. They produced terrific products that fit with emerging life-styles. For the first five years, profits kept getting better and better. Then they hit the wall. Sales went flat, competitors made inroads, morale plummetted. The company's founders couldn't figure out what had happened.

I met with them and asked some questions: What did you think about before you created your products? Is your market primarily business or consumer? What are your customers' demographics and psychographics? Have you found your business to be seasonally or geographically influenced? How has the business changed over the years? Where do you hope to be five years from now, and how do you intend to get there?

There were many more questions. They had very few answers.

It wasn't that they didn't know their products and their market. They just didn't know them well enough. It didn't mean failure, but it was a big disadvantage.

The Wholistic Way

All of this boils down to big-picture thinking. Organizations have to provide the big picture to everyone: employees, suppliers, the media, analysts, themselves.

Access to the big picture is gained through constant questioning and searching for answers.

This takes time, energy and effort. It requires more than internal training programs. It begins at the top, with a commitment to an open-door policy and superior communication. And it never ends. In good times and bad, in crisis situations and in periods of high profits, a company must keep the information flowing.

The result will be a company driven by motivation, enthusiasm, inspiration and leadership.

CHAPTER FOURTEEN

Leadership: More Than Titles and Power

Leadership is a loaded word. Like justice, equality and freedom, everyone believes in it, but few can agree on its meaning.

To one person, leadership means decision-making.

To another, it signifies absolute authority.

To yet another, it connotes setting direction.

Beyond its many meanings, there's the question of how to obtain it. Can it be learned or is it innate? Are leaders born or bred?

There's also the concept of leadership styles. Autocratic leaders versus humanistic ones, a flamboyant style versus a conservative one.

From my experience as a manager and a CEO, I've learned a great deal about leadership. My views on the subject are probably different than most. First, leaders have to be dreamers. The CEO who runs the largest corporation in America but whose vision doesn't extend beyond the next profit-and-loss statement isn't a leader; he's an accountant. The manager who terrifies his people into working harder and longer than everyone else isn't a leader; he's a dictator.

Leadership is the sum of many positive parts. It's an accumulation of attributes, the development of numerous attitudes, talents and skills. Just as most people have the capacity to dream, most have the ability to become leaders. They all won't be the same types of leaders; each will have his or her own style. But they'll all share certain traits.

What are those traits? How can they be acquired? What does leadership mean to an organization and what happens when it's absent?

Let's examine those and other questions.

Two Types of Managers

Titles don't make leaders. A CEO isn't necessarily a leader. A junior executive might be.

There's a big difference between managers and leaders; there are managers, and there are manager-leaders.

A manager is a technician, a practicing specialist. He's like a plumber or carpenter who knows all the requirements for getting the job done. But that doesn't make him a leader. Some managers are content only to be managers, lacking the motivation to reach higher.

A manager-leader, however, is another species. He or she is a risk-taker—not a gambler, but one who is willing to take calculated risks. Leaders aren't intimidated by failure. Managers are. When managers make mistakes, their future decisions are affected by those mistakes. A shipping manager tells one of his people to send a shipment of goods to a warehouse in New Orleans. His subordinate accidentally sends it to New York. That causes all sorts of problems, and the shipping manager gets chewed out by his boss. From that point on, the manager is reluctant to delegate any important decisions to subordinates.

The manager-leader reacts differently. He's careful not to make the same mistake twice, but he's not intimidated by his failure. He firmly believes that progress is made only by taking measurable risks, that you have to take some risk if you want to move forward.

A manager-leader sees the big picture. He can dream; he has a vision. A manager tends to look at things with a narrow perspective, viewing his job within the framework of his assignment and his tools to accomplish it.

Organizations should take it upon themselves to help managers become manager-leaders. There's no such thing as too many leaders. The more leaders a company has, the better able it will be to institute change, deal with crises, and increase work-force morale.

A Profile in Leadership

What qualities should leaders strive for?

Let's begin with a positive attitude. Naysayers aren't leaders. Neither are wafflers who refuse to make commitments. You've got to be an optimist; you have to figure you can succeed despite the odds.

Speaking of odds, a leader doesn't wait to do something until the odds of success are almost 100 percent. It's astonishing how many companies won't embark on a new course until they consider that direction a sure thing. They'll keep trying to improve the odds in their favor, wasting time and money. By the time they've reached that optimal point, it's often too late. They wait and wait to introduce a new product until they're positive that everything's right for the introduction, and by that time their competitors have a head start.

A leader feels lucky. It's part and parcel of his positive outlook. He feels in his gut that things will work out. The things that others see as obstacles he views as opportunities; he just knows that he'll be able to surmount them.

It's a self-fulfilling prophecy: If you feel lucky, you are lucky. In more formal terms, it translates into confidence. Leaders aren't foolishly confident but they have a bedrock certainty about their actions.

A leader doesn't sweat the details. He's concerned with the big picture. He doesn't confuse strategy with details.

137

People at Spiegel would often come to me and say, "We can do that." I'd respond, "But if we could do it, would it help us?" They'd say, "Yes, but it costs too much money." Or "Sure, but we don't have the equipment to make it work."

"Those are details," I'd explain. "Details can be overcome."

Imagine the engineers who built the railroad tracks that made opening the West possible. What if they had come across a big gorge and said, "Well, we can't get across that, we might as well go home." They realized it was just a detail. They were driven by a powerful vision, and it allowed them to eliminate the problematic details.

A leader is a doer. He doesn't just have responsibility; he likes responsibility. He doesn't merely accept his assignments; he takes the initiative to create new assignments.

When I was a kid, I played on a sandlot baseball team. Our games were early Saturday morning, and that created a problem. Although everyone wanted to play, nobody particularly wanted to wake everyone else up and get them out to the field.

I took that responsibility. I went from house to house shouting for them to get up and meet at the field. I liked doing it. After a while, my fellow ballplayers expected me to do it. They started looking at me as the organizer, as the leader.

A leader does things because he wants to get things done. A true leader doesn't do them because he's insecure and worried what others will think if he sits on his hands.

Leaders are evangelists, communicators, motivators. Leaders make disciples through the force of their will and their visions and their abilities to express their dreams.

Leaders Versus Followers

Just because you're in a leadership position doesn't mean you automatically lead. There are times when you'll be confronted with situations where you'll be tempted to follow another's course rather than the one your instinct tells you to choose. Your leadership ability will often be tested.

I remember when I was flying on a mission in Europe during World War II. We took off from England in miserable weather, overcast and rainy up to 20,000 feet. There were about thirty planes in our group, and normally we'd assemble over England. But because of the weather, we decided to fly beyond England and assemble at a designated point over France. I was a pilot, and as I was taking us through the soup I asked Don O'Brien, my navigator, what our heading was. He told me 60 degrees right. I veered off in that direction.

"Hey, wait a second, Hank," my co-pilot said. "Everybody else is going off at 30 degrees, we better follow them." Sure enough, the planes in front of us were all taking a different course than we were. But I stayed on the course that Don had told me was right.

"What are you doing, Hank?" my co-pilot shouted in alarm. "We're going to get lost!"

"What makes you think the guys you want me to follow know where they're going?" I asked him. "Do you have more confidence in those fellows you don't even know instead of Don, who you know is a good navigator?"

"You're making a big mistake," my co-pilot grumbled.

Well, it turned out we came right up on the formation over France, and ten planes were missing. I never forgot the lesson I learned: You've got to have confidence in your instincts, even if everyone else is telling you you're wrong. If you have good instincts—and it's something leaders must have—more often than not you'll be right.

Leadership Styles

Like snowflakes, no two leaders are alike. Each will have a different personality, and that means a different leadership style.

I've seen leaders who were flamboyant and controversial, who loved the limelight and had egos big as the great outdoors. I've seen other leaders who were more reserved, who led by example rather than by grandstanding.

There's no one leadership style that fits all. But there are styles that have become outmoded or are simply inappropriate.

An example of the former is the autocratic leader. Everyone's heard the stories about CEOs who ruled their companies with iron fists, tolerating no dissent, intimidating anyone who crossed their paths. Today, few employees will tolerate such a leader. They're better educated, more sophisticated; they also have more options. They'll respond to that autocratic leader by leaving the organization at the first opportunity or become brown-nosers and conformists, never operating at maximum ability.

A leader wants his people to be risk-takers, but he'll never achieve that goal if he threatens and belittles. You can't get someone to take a risk by putting him or her at risk.

I don't think there are many, if any, leaders who are introverted and uncommunicative. It's fine to have people like that in a company; they may be excellent at their jobs and contribute a great deal. But a leader can't afford to wall himself off from his subordinates and think great thoughts to himself. Like a politician, he's got to be out there beating the bushes, trying to convince the masses that his vision is the right one.

On the positive side, humanists make the best leaders. Compassion, ethics, sensitivity to others are all valuable traits. The cynical might say that such traits have no place in the dog-eat-dog world of business. I think those cynics don't truly understand leadership.

I'm not saying that a leader should be a soft touch. A leader is the boss, and he should command respect. But employees rarely give respect to a manager who treats them like dirt.

There are going to be times when a manager has to chew out an employee when he or she does something wrong. I had to call people on the carpet a number of times. But after I was done with my critique, I countered it with support and encouragement. My policy was that no one would leave my office feeling bad. I firmly believe that criticism is a true learning experience when it's leavened with the positive.

In fact, I tried to maintain a humanistic approach to all aspects of corporate life at Spiegel. At many companies, when someone leaves (usually for another job, often at a competitor), management's attitude toward the departing employee is that he or she is persona non grata. Such an approach is not only unfeeling, it's counterproductive. Whenever a valuable executive left Spiegel, I'd take her into my office and say, "I'm sorry you're leaving. You've been a valuable contributor and I hate to see you go. If things don't work out, I want you to call me, and if it's possible, I'll try to find a place for you back here."

Some did come back. In almost every case, those who returned were more valuable employees than before. Not only had they acquired additional skills, but they responded with great enthusiasm to a second chance with the company.

Leadership style should fit the company's situation and needs. Spiegel needed my style of leadership. They needed an evangelical leader with vision and a highly aggressive, risk-taking approach. A more conservative leadership style wouldn't have been sufficient to lift the company out of its doldrums.

On the other hand, my style might have been wrong for a different type of company. If I were installed as CEO of Sears, I might have been less effective than a more disciplined, more conservative chief executive.

Encouraging Managers to Become Manager-Leaders

The majority of managers have leadership potential. Certainly there are a minority who can't become leaders. For one reason or another, they just don't have what it takes. Some people will always be followers. Others don't have the necessary intelligence or temperment.

But most managers can become manager-leaders if top management provides them with the opportunity and incentives to do so. It's not just through leadership training programs that managers grow. It is through example, attitude and motivation. Are the CEO and his top officers manager-leaders or managers? Do they encourage managers to become leaders? The leadership potential of hundreds of managers in a given organization will lie dormant if they don't have the incentive to bring it out.

How can an organization provide the incentive? Every company will have its own methods. I realize that's a very simple answer, but it's important to understand that leadership is as much an art as a science, and that no one formula works for all.

When I was at Spiegel, my method was to provide every employee with as much freedom as possible to be a leader. No one was afraid to suggest a new idea because it would be ignored or they'd be punished if it didn't work out. I organized the company in a way that titles meant as little as possible; the middle managers were given far more responsibility than at other companies. I put everyone on a level playing field—everyone understood Spiegel's dream and had a chance to contribute to the realization of that dream. I rewarded those who understood the big picture and helped bring it about. Those who did well at Spiegel were leaders; financially and careerwise, the people who ascended were those who were out front, actively taking calculated risks, inspiring subordinates and enthusiastically pursuing the dream.

The Leadership Checklist

How can you chart your course from manager to manager-leader? How can you determine if you're moving in the right direction?

142

One way is to have a checklist—a checklist of leadership qualities that you can examine to figure out if you're on the right track.

Take a look at the following list of questions and consider your answers.

1. Do you look at the big picture or do you get hung up on details?

2. Are you willing to take risks?

3. Are you intimidated by failure?

4. Do you follow the pack or do you break off in the direction you think is best?

5. Are your actions motivated by a larger vision or by the narrow requirements of your job?

6. Are you a caring, compassionate, ethical manager?

7. Do you feel lucky and confident?

8. Are you a positive thinker or do you let doubts and uncertainties turn you into a naysayer?

9. Do you communicate clearly, convincingly and inspirationally?

10. Does your enthusiasm and energy turn others into believers in the company's goals and dreams?

Ask yourself these questions regularly. Keep tabs on your leadership qualities. If you find yourself lacking in one area, resolve to improve.

It's not as hard as it might seem. You don't have to be a genius to be a manager-leader. You don't have to study and learn vast amounts of new information. What it boils down to is drawing upon your positive traits—qualities you might have ignored or failed to nurture. To be a leader, you have to think like one. My checklist is a way to make that process a little easier.

Leadership and the Dream

Everything I've said about leadership goes double if you're embarking on a corporate dream strategy. Dreams are fragile things. They require leaders to hold all the disparate pieces together.

Imagine a company striving to remake itself. Perhaps it's an organization that is about to launch a revolutionary new product. Or perhaps it's a company that has implemented a radical approach to customer service. Or maybe it's a corporation that is trying to sell its customers on a new technology. Whatever the scenario, the company has a vision.

Every vision, every dream, invites controversy and criticism. Because the idea is new and requires change, there will be those—both inside and outside of the company—who say it can't or shouldn't be done. Boards of directors, the media, security analysts, the company's own executives—some of these groups will put up a fight.

Without strong leadership, the company will lose the fight. The dream will break apart as the snipers hit undefended targets.

The autocratic CEO will catalyze fear rather than loyalty. His dictatorial style will prevent him from inspiring corporate-wide belief in the dream.

The company composed of managers rather than manager-leaders will have department heads that lack initiative. They will await instructions rather than forging ahead on their own. The dream will die while they wait.

The chief executive unable to communicate effectively will be unable to translate his dream into vibrant, understandable terms.

The vice presidents who second-guess themselves, who don't feel lucky, won't be willing to take the risks a dream demands.

Dream strategies thrive in an environment where leadership qualities are in abundance. The more risk-taking, motivation, communication, compassion and positive thinking there is, the more likely the dream strategy will succeed.

CHAPTER FIFTEEN

Managing Relationships

Relationships between superiors, subordinates and peers within an organization can be managed. In fact, they should be managed. Every executive should be aware not only of his or her role within the company, but of how he or she can best work with a variety of other people.

Why is this important? Because a company can only go so far with its products and services, its strategies and tactics. People make everything work. If a company has individuals who don't get along with their bosses or bosses who treat their subordinates with disrespect or peers who engage in one-upmanship to get ahead, then the company will fall short of its dream.

A number of issues influence employee relationships. Let's start with the "difficult" boss.

Adapting to the Boss

You join a company with great expectations. You love the business, the job description sounds great, you bring tremendous energy and enthusiasm to the company.

After a few months, all the energy and enthusiasm are gone. Frequently, the culprit is your relationship with your boss. You can't stand him. You feel he's arrogant, insensitive, unappreciative—choose an adjective.

I've seen it happen hundreds of times. Many times, the problem lies not with the boss, but with the subordinate. You don't get to choose your boss. It's not the boss's responsibility to adapt to each of his subordinates. For better or worse, as long as he's the boss and you're the employee, you are going to have to be the one making the adjustment.

A great many bright, young, well-educated employees don't agree. Years ago, things were different. Then, companies were more like the military: you shaped up or shipped out. You followed orders, no matter how they were issued or how wrong-headed you might perceive them to be.

People coming into the workplace today have different attitudes. Their life-style and education have encouraged them to question orders, to be defiant in the face of authority, to be individuals. They don't adapt to their bosses' idiosyncracies, prejudices and personality. Instead, they fight them. The result is resentment and confrontations that hurt everyone's productivity.

Don't get me wrong: you don't have to be a slave. But you do have to find a middle ground where you maintain your self-respect but also adjust to your boss.

People complain that their bosses are "impossible." That's rare. Difficult, yes. Usually, the difficulties are related to small things. He may place a higher priority on matters that you feel are trivial.

For instance, he's a stickler for punctuality. If you're one minute late for work, he chews you out. Rather than fight him on the issue, get to work on time. For whatever reason, it's important to him, and it doesn't take much effort to do what he asks.

Learn your boss's hot buttons. Figure out what ticks him off, what pleases him. Do things his way, even if you believe his way is wrong. Give your boss a chance. Odds are, a few years down the road, you'll look back and realize he wasn't so bad, and maybe some of the things he espoused made sense.

There are limits, of course. If your boss is a true ogre, if he really does treat you like a slave, then quit. But quitting is a last resort and before you exercise that option, try to work with him. Avoid trying to work around him—going behind his back or over his head to get things accomplished. It will only lower your productivity and create resentment.

Who Gets the Credit

One thing that really galls people is a superior who takes credit for their idea. You come up with a great idea for restructuring your division and tell your boss about it. His response is positive, but he cautions you that he has to run it by his boss. In a division meeting a little while later, you are aghast to hear your boss's boss complimenting him on his well-thought-out plan to restructure his group.

It's irritating. Your immediate impulse is to confront your superior and berate him for stealing your idea. If you do that, you are not managing your relationship properly. What you're doing is letting your ego dictate your relationship with a superior. It was T.S. Eliot who once said that bad poets borrow; good poets steal. Translated to a business environment, that means no idea is really an original one. If your supervisor steals your idea, so what? As long as it helps the company, what does it matter whose idea
it is?

Your goal is to earn your boss's respect and trust. By giving him ideas that make him look good in the eyes of his boss, you're doing just that. Ultimately, you'll be rewarded. As your value to him increases, you'll receive the promotions, assignments and salary increases that are your due.

Don't think short-term. Think of yourself as a baseball player who gets five hundred at bats, not one. If you have to sacrifice the runner along rather than try and hit a home run, so be it. The team will benefit, and your contribution will be acknowledged. As you gain stature within the organization, you'll be given plenty of chances to swing for the fences.

Changing Relationships

At Aldens, I had a boss who was a pain in the neck. He was pompous, arbitrary and insecure. On more than one occasion, I heard him laying claim to ideas that were mine, not his.

I did everything possible to accommodate him. For instance, he was indecisive, postponing important decisions as long as possible, putting projects in jeopardy. Rather than tell him that his indecision was wrong and hurt the company, I took another approach. Sometimes, I'd fashion elaborate presentations which I knew would impress him; he loved dog and pony shows, and I recognized he was more likely to make a decision if all the stops were pulled out when presenting.

My boss was also late for meetings. He seemed to enjoy making his subordinates wait, forcing us to sit and twiddle our thumbs until he was willing to make his entrance. The problem, of course, was that when he finally arrived, we didn't have enough time to accomplish what we wanted. So I devised schemes to get him to meetings on time. I'd tell him how important his presence was at the meeting, explaining that we needed *his* input and advice or our plan wouldn't work. Or I'd arrange for a VIP to be at the meeting, telling my boss in advance that a bigshot was coming.

Over time, his attitude toward me changed. As I adapted to him, he adapted to me. Because I had taken the first steps, he responded in kind. He began to trust and depend on me. When I presented an idea, he was no longer as indecisive or arrogant as he had been. The result was that our department had one success after another. He needed me and I needed him, and that realization allowed us to move to a common ground.

No question, there were times that I just wanted to let him have it. His peculiar ideas about management were exasperating. But I avoided the blow-ups that would have doomed our relationship.

It's critical to avoid no-holds-barred arguments. The bad taste lingers in both the boss's and subordinate's mouths long after it's over.

Instead of arguing, present. Instead of rushing into the boss's office and protesting, "What you're saying doesn't make any sense," try, "Let's take a look at it another way," or "I admit you're right about that point, but let's take a look at what the benefits will be if we can overcome that obstacle."

Many managers instinctively look at both sides of every issue. For every positive you bring up, they'll bring up a negative. It's going to happen and you can't prevent it. What you can do is not have a fit about those negatives. Pose a hypothetical situation: "What if we could find a way to deal with those negatives? Would it be worth it to go ahead based on the idea's positive attributes? If it works, think how much it will mean to us." You must gently push a negative-thinking boss to the positive side. It can't be done through confrontation and argument. It can be done through friendly persuasion.

Relationships from the Boss's Perspective

It's a two-way street. The best companies manage relationships "up and down."

Why should the boss have to manage relationships with his subordinates? After all, it's the responsibility of the subordinate to adapt to his superior, not the other way around.

Let me put it this way. A boss can do things which make it easier for his people to adapt. He can set the tone for his division, his group—a tone that is positive or negative. The best managers do more than manage the business; they make an effort to consider the needs, problems and potential of each person in the group, and by that effort increase the value of each and every employee.

Avoid Yes or No Situations

The boss who resorts to black-and-white, either/or answers is doing a disservice to his subordinates. Don't fool yourself into thinking you're being decisive. Instead, you're making people dependent on you, robbing them of the responsibility and accountability they should have.

To avoid putting my people in yes-or-no situations, I rarely made snap judgments that ended discussions. If someone told me about a new project she wanted to pursue, I'd ask: What did she think we should do? What were the risks and opportunities? Did she think we should go ahead? If she said she thought we should move forward, I'd usually say go ahead. I wanted her to take the responsibility; I didn't want her to come back later when it failed and say, "Well, I cleared it with you first."

Sometimes, of course, I couldn't let someone go ahead because of financial or other considerations. But I didn't kill the idea with an absolute no. Instead, I'd give the idea's sponsor a reasonable time frame to marshal an argument in the idea's favor. If that person really felt strongly, he'd come up with sufficient facts that would allow him to proceed.

There are two clear benefits to this management approach. First, it avoids subordinates walking into your office and walking out feeling devastated if you say no. Second, it prevents them from shifting all responsibility from their shoulders to yours.

Taking the Time

"The boss can't see you until next Friday."

Many managers get all wound up in their schedules. This is especially true for upper-level managers, who often have aides

152

who take the responsibility for scheduling. If you've worked for a large company, you've seen these aides: they often jealously guard their boss's time, refusing all requests for earlier appointments, despite the fervent pleas of a subordinate for "just a minute."

It's a harmful practice. The manager who is unavailable to his people is not managing his relationships properly. If he's booked solid for two weeks with major meetings and can't find the time for other things, those other things won't get done. He becomes isolated, walled off from his subordinates by an intimidating, unbending schedule.

I had a policy designed to circumvent this problem at Spiegel. I told everyone, including my secretary, that if you need an answer to something that will allow you to progress—and if it won't take more than a few minutes—call me and I'll interrupt whatever meeting I'm in.

This policy didn't meet with universal approval. A number of people groused that they could never get me to sit down and listen without an interruption, and to a certain extent, that was true. But it was much more preferable than the alternative. My feeling was and is that you have to be responsive to your employees—all of your employees, not only the top-level ones. Just because you're in a meeting, why should you shut everything else out? No reason, except that it's awkward to have interruptions.

You must keep things moving. Every day, your subordinates will have questions, concerns and problems, and you're in the best position to handle them. If you delay the resolution of an issue for a week, that means a week wasted. Multiply that by fifty issues in a given month and it exacts a toll, both on the company and on your relationship with each employee who can't get through to you. So make sure your people understand that you're willing to talk to them, no matter what you're doing; that if they feel the matter is important and they require a few minutes, you'll give it to them. Take the time—it's a win-win deal.

Confidence and Responsibility

One of the best things a manager can do for his people is to communicate his confidence in them and back up his words by giving them real responsibility.

One without the other won't work. If you give a subordinate a big job and then say, "You better not screw this up," then you're inviting disaster. Similarly, if you encourage someone but fail to give her a meaty job she can sink her teeth into, you've also failed.

It's going to be easier to give responsibility and confidence to certain employees—the ones who always seem to come through for you when you give them an assignment. It's okay to have favorites; it's human nature to do so. At the same time, however, don't neglect others who might have the potential to become stars.

Don't always give an important assignment to the top guy in your department. Offer the opportunity to someone lower down the ladder for a change. Also, try giving the same task to two different people. As long as you don't position the assignment in a cutthroat way—winner take all—then you'll have healthy competition and you'll be able to spread choice assignments around.

Rewards

To a certain extent, your relationship with subordinates depends on their financial compensation. If someone feels you haven't given him the salary increase or bonus he deserves, he will not be particularly motivated to do an outstanding job.

I've already talked about bonuses, so I won't belabor the point here. However, you'll recall that I called for bonuses to be distributed in proportion to how the company does. Let me add something to that idea. Some companies do adhere to this concept, but they tie bonuses to corporate goals that are far too high. Therefore, when the company's performance falls short of objectives, everyone is disappointed and loses motivation.

It's far wiser to have achievable goals—goals that everyone agrees are realistic. If the company falls short of those goals, people won't feel slighted. Instead, they'll admit they didn't get the job done or economic and competitive factors caused them to fall short. If objectives are met, on the other hand, every contributor benefits—not just the top-level people, but anyone who makes daily decisions that influence the company's performance.

People Working with People

Imagine a company where everyone is working together for the greater corporate good, where all the diverse personalities within the organization blend smoothly, where instead of bitter rivalries there's healthy competition, where people are excited about their peers' successes, where political game-playing is at a minimum and no one resents a fellow employee's triumphs.

This is the ideal atmosphere for managing relationships among peers. Contrary to what some cynics might say, it's an achievable ideal.

At Spiegel, we were close to it. No, we couldn't eliminate politics entirely, especially at the lower managerial levels. Some people did resent it when co-workers received promotions they thought should have been theirs. But, overall, the people at Spiegel worked wonderfully together. Our employees respected one another. They cooperated and compromised willingly. They put the company ahead of the individual. They set aside individual differences to accomplish larger objectives. There were relatively few complaints about favoritism. Personality clashes were few and far between. People rooted for each other like members of an athletic team.

155

All this was possible because of Spiegel's dream. It linked everyone together. We all had a common cause. All the pettiness and bickering were swept aside as the dream took shape. There was the realization that if we could bring the dream to life, everyone would share in it. It was a powerful reason for employees to find a way to work with each other for the sake of the corporate dream.

In a way, it was like a circus. Imagine an empty field. Think about the circus arriving in their trucks and wagons and the people pouring out, pounding stakes into the ground, hoisting the big tents, performers practicing their routines, the animals being led to their cages, the diverse cast of clowns, roughnecks, trapeze artists and acrobats engaged in their specialized activities.

The field is transformed by the circus, and the transformation is magical. Hundreds of disparate people with diverse skills come together to create a single entertainment.

The circus people take tremendous pride in their work. If you talk to one and ask them what they do, they'll puff out their chests and say, "I'm with the circus."

It was the same way at Spiegel. When our people had to work overtime to meet a deadline, no one complained; no one felt like they were being taken advantage of. The dream made such complaints beside the point. They knew what they were working toward. If something didn't work, no one wasted time coming up with excuses for why it failed; they just buckled down and tried to create a viable alternative.

Visit a circus the day before it opens. You'll see an incredible amount of activity. People are rushing this way and that, tacking up signs, practicing their acts, setting up stands. You can sense how excited they are. If you ask them why they're running to and fro, they'll look at you and say, "The circus opens tomorrow," as if there couldn't be a better explanation.

It was that way at Spiegel. Everyone, in his or her own way, was working on a part of the dream. And if you were to stop one of them as he rushed through the hallways and asked him what was the hurry, he'd look at you and say, ''The catalog comes out tomorrow.''

Spiegel was a great place to work. It was a place where relationships between peers were excellent. Who managed those relationships? Not the CEO or the individual managers. It was the dream, our common vision of Spiegel's future. Any company that creates and communicates such a vision won't have to worry about disgruntled employees or game-playing. People will take the responsibility for working together, for adjusting to one another.

CHAPTER SIXTEEN

The Customer

It wasn't so long ago that customers were relatively passive. They accepted substandard products and marginal service. They put up with automobiles that broke down after a few years and with rude, uninformed salespeople.

No more. Customers have become more demanding. They won't stand for service or products that fall below their increasingly high expectations.

This new attitude is a result of communications. People are better informed than in the past. The media have done an excellent job of raising their awareness of quality. People are encouraged to complain if something doesn't work or doesn't arrive on time or to switch their loyalties (and purchases) from one company to another.

This is especially true for the top one-third of households—the upper-middle-class, well-educated, two-income households that have the majority of this country's discretionary income. For many companies, they are the key to success. If you don't satisfy them with superior products and service, you lose them.

Priorities

The following is the order of priorities for many organizations: themselves, their companies, their customers.

That is the wrong order. Organizations that put their customers third rarely finish first. How can they, when they're more concerned with their own perks and salaries and the company's status than with satisfying their customers.

When I came to Spiegel, our priorities were wrong. We were suspicious of our credit-dependent customers; we thought, "They're trying to get something for nothing." We didn't respect the intelligence of our customers, and our marketing reflected that disrespect, employing puffery and exaggeration rather than convincing, informative facts. Our products and services were barely adequate.

Like many companies, we felt a standardized approach was fine. We didn't tailor our products and services to meet the specific needs of our customers. A coat is a coat is a coat: there was no impetus for us to offer a coat that was different, that was exactly right for a Spiegel customer.

Companies that adhere to this standardized concept are doomed. The common-denominator idea is hopelessly old-fashioned. It is a result of customer-third thinking.

Customers Respond to Newness

If you're a big, established company—even if you're a market leader—you're at a serious disadvantage. You are now or soon will be competing against new companies—companies with dreams and niches, unburdened by tradition or bigness.

Customers love new things—new companies and their fresh ideas and ways of doing business. That is why a company like WalMart has been so successful, even though it's competing against giants like Sears. They can introduce stores that are tailored to the times, to the life-styles, economics and needs of a targeted group of consumers.

They also have the advantage of distribution economies—the way they present, stack and pack. Older companies can't match these new systems. At best, companies like Sears and K Mart can try to restructure their stores and systems. But they're forced to play catch-up, and no matter what they do, customers will view them as old and WalMart as new.

The future belongs to the new niche marketers, the organizations that aren't trying to be all things to all people. Customers respond with overwhelming enthusiasm to niche marketers who have dreams.

Companies that stake out their own narrow piece of turf and dominate it are winners. People are naturally going to be attracted to this type of company. A company that does what it does better than anyone—that offers a customer more product and service choices—has a great shot at success.

The big market leaders are vulnerable to niche marketers. No matter how large an organization is, no matter how great its resources, it cannot compete with a niche marketer who inevitably offers its customers greater quality and choice. They can dazzle customers with their new dream, promising them a better way. It is a powerful argument, and one that few large, diversified corporations can counter.

Excuses

Customers don't care about excuses.

Corporations don't always see it that way. They often look at their customer failures as explainable, excusable. They're like families where two siblings point at each other and say, "He did it!" Or like kids who look at their parents and explain the eight different reasons why they weren't able to get their homework done on time.

No one is perfect. Every company is going to have situations where they fail customers. But those situations can be few and far between with the right philosophy—a philosophy that refuses to tolerate excuses.

It is not that the excuses aren't legitimate. Trucks break down on the way to the warehouse. A supplier promises you something that he is unable to deliver. The computer system is down. The customer didn't fill out the form correctly.

There are thousands of excuses. But if you use them as a scapegoat for poor customer service, the company will be in trouble. A customer waiting for his package to arrive doesn't care whose fault it is that the delivery is late.

You have to find a way around the problems to satisfy customers. All it takes is some imagination and initiative. It requires an honest desire to provide the customer with what he expects from you.

When I arrived at Spiegel, excuses were epidemic. One person would say, I can't do this because of so and so. Another person wouldn't be able to accomplish her job because of the first person. A third employee wouldn't be able to achieve an objective because of the second person. One excuse led to another. The cumulative effect was to hog-tie everyone. In a culture that condones excuses, it doesn't seem so bad to rely on them.

Ultimately, both the customer and the company suffer.

Spiegel eliminated the excuse mentality. Instead of blaming someone for a problem, we found alternative solutions. If a source couldn't be counted on to provide us with products on a timely basis, we'd find another source. If a customer complained she was expecting a package that didn't arrive, we'd pull out all the stops to get her that package.

There are all sorts of ways to solve a problem. If the traditional way doesn't work, find another one. If a company can communicate this to employees—that everyone is responsible and accountable to the customer, and that it's up to each employee to find methods ensuring responsibility and accountability—then the number of excuses will drop dramatically.

It's Not What You Sell but How You Serve It Up

Products don't sell themselves. Unless you have one of those rare and wonderful "breakthroughs," customers aren't going to beat a path to your door. In most cases, you're competing on equal footing with others.

What then? How do you capture the customer?

With service that saves the customer time.

To understand the power of efficient service, you don't have to look further than the phenomenon of self-serve gas stations.

Ten years ago, who would have thought that pumping one's own gas would become so popular? The lower cost is part of the reason, but there is a bigger concept involved.

Look at the evolution of the self-serve stations. At first, they just converted a few pumps to self-serve. Then they added a few other non-gas, self-serve conveniences like equipment for you to clean your windows, add oil and fill up your tires with air. Soon, a new breed of gas station emerged—total self-serve stations, huge places with row upon row of self-serve islands.

It's been an evolution of increasing efficiency. Self-serve stations save customers time. There's no waiting for someone else to do all the things you can do faster.

As I've stated before, people are busier than ever before. If you can find a way to save them time—even only seconds or minutes—you will have a happy and loyal customer base. It's happening in all marketplace segments—ten-minute oil changes, drive-up windows in fast-food establishments (making fast food even faster), overnight mail services.

Customers are willing to pay for speed. It costs far more to use Federal Express than to send a package by regular mail. This is not to say people aren't price-conscious, but don't make the mistake of thinking that today's customer buys on price alone. They don't want cheaper things. They want better things cheaper.

Big difference! They're looking for value. Even people who don't have a great deal of money buy Reeboks. Of course, they'll search long and hard for the retailer who gives them the best price. But they'll still pay more for a quality brand than a cheap imitation.

Service Is More Than a Smile

When companies talk about service, they talk about courteous, informed salespeople; about efficiency and speed; about answering customer complaints promptly. All those things are important. But customers view service from a broader perspective.

For example, I have difficulty finding shoes to fit my large, narrow feet. When choosing a shoe store, I look for a place that carries quality brands at reasonable prices. I appreciate a salesperson who is knowledgeable and pleasant.

But more important than anything else, I want a store that carries my size of shoe. If I go into a store and they don't carry my size, that's poor service. If the salesperson tells me, "I'm sorry, we don't have that size, it's a slow-selling one, we get so few requests for it," I look at him and say, "I'm here. I want it. If you don't have it, I'm not coming back. And I'm not going to bring my wife and daughter back, either."

Real service is giving the customer exactly what he or she wants. No amount of courtesy or speed is an adequate substitute if you don't meet that service requirement.

Companies must do a better job of defining customer expectations. What do your customers really want? What ticks them off? What makes them happy? Go beyond the superficial things to what really counts. Are they irritated because certain items are always out of stock? Is it important to them that someone be available if they have questions about a product? Do they find your bills to be confusing?

Don't assume you know what the customer wants. Your definition of service and theirs may be worlds apart.

Service with Compassion

How do your customers feel about your company? About your products and services?

A customer doesn't have to care about how you feel, but you have every obligation to consider a customer's feelings.

Some organizations consider their customers pains in the rear end. They might not come out and say it, but they think it. Reacting to some snafu, they think, "What's the matter with these people? This is going to be a real mess. I've got better things to do than deal with these petty problems."

Customers' problems aren't petty. If you ignore those problems or treat them lightly, you risk alienating your customers. You don't want them to feel as I do when a shoe store doesn't have my size.

Empathize! Hire people who have compassion for customers. Form a group of service people with a mandate to take the customers' side. As I mentioned in an earlier chapter, we did exactly that at Spiegel, and it greatly enhanced our customer relationships. Even though they were Spiegel employees, they fought for our customers. And they were given the power to fight effectively. If a customer called saying she was upset about something, these customer advocates wouldn't make excuses. They'd take the customer's side and find a way to solve the problem.

Service with compassion means making more than a philosophical commitment. It means spending money on things that don't directly result in increased profits. General Electric is a company that has taken this step. They've spent millions of dollars on a toll-free hotline for customers' questions about their products. They've staffed what they call the "Answer Line" with sharp, well-informed people who have the resources to find answers for callers. General Electric can talk all they want about how they're a company that cares because the hotline backs up the talk with action.

What happens, though, if times get tough? What if G.E.'s profits go down or there's a recession? Will the numbers guys look at the cost of the hotline and wonder if it's worth the expense? I think it's worth it in spades. You don't exchange compassionate service for short-term profits. If you do, you've made a bad trade.

Monitoring Customer Relationships

The image and attitude customers have about your company can change quickly. In fact, it is most vulnerable to change after they've purchased your product or service, not before.

During this time, things can go wrong: the product fails, a customer service representative is rude or unhelpful, the process to fix or replace the failed product irritates the customer or takes too long.

Companies often don't monitor the changing relationships caused by post-sale problems. They incorrectly assume that the system they have in place will work fine without monitoring. As a result, customer relationships deteriorate.

Monitoring relationships isn't difficult; it just takes procedures that ensure follow-up communication between company and customer.

I recently had a problem with my trash compactor. A repairman came to my house, examined the compactor and found there was a problem with a switch. Unfortunately, he didn't have the part with him to fix it there and then. I asked him if he thought it was good service to take the compactor apart and not have the replacement switch required to make it work. He agreed it wasn't but assured me that he'd have it next time; he arranged a time and date to return. He came back and fixed the compactor.

The next day, I received a call from the company asking me if the repair was satisfactory. I said it was fine, although I wished the repairman had the part required on the first visit. The company representative told me she'd make a note of my complaint and they would try to avoid that problem in the future.

That's what I call monitoring customer relationships.

The Dream Customer

Imagine the ideal customer. When your company's name is mentioned, she automatically responds positively. She praises your products and service to her friends. When it comes to a buying decision, she'll choose your company's products more often than not, regardless of price. If something goes wrong with the product, she feels confident that she can make one call and get the problem remedied.

This ideal customer isn't found; she's cultivated by you. I've outlined a number of tactics to "make" this customer. If you're a corporate dreamer, they'll be a natural part of your strategy.

Corporate dreams, by definition, put the customer first. They work from the outside in, targeting a market segment first and creating products (or services) designed exclusively for that segment. Service with compassion and efficiency, monitoring customer relationships, no excuses for failures and niche marketing approaches are all part of the dream.

During my years at Spiegel, I watched our customers change as we changed. As we put our dream into motion, customers responded. They became a part of it. Make your customers part of your dream and you'll have countless ideal customers.

CHAPTER SEVENTEEN

Marketing

Marketing theories are numerous, as are the catchy names describing those theories: maximarketing, micromarketing, marketing warfare.

My theory about marketing is simple. It doesn't require a genius to understand it or a huge budget to implement it. It worked at Spiegel and it has worked for hundreds of other companies. It revolves around the most powerful marketing approach ever created, one that can overcome any obstacle. It cuts through the clutter, it ensures customer loyalty, and it creates superior image and awareness.

To me, marketing means getting the customer to love you: your company, your products, your service—and above all else, your dream. If you convince others to fall in love with your dream, you will have done the best selling job possible.

Messengers of Love

One of the ways you can get customers to love you is through advertising.

They won't love you, however, if your advertising is merely clever, visually dazzling or even brilliant. It has to be more than that, and you can't depend on the intuitive abilities of your advertising department or the talented writers in your ad agency to achieve the goal.

Before you create your advertising, you have to know what your target audience's concerns are relative to your product or service. Don't assume you know. The assumptions you make are often at odds with your market's true feelings.

Research is crucial. At Spiegel, we assumed our ads should feature our new, designer-name fashions. We figured that our target audience's primary concern was whether Spiegel carried the hot names they were looking for.

But we did some research, and what it told us was surprising. What worried our target audience most, the one thing that made them hesitate before purchasing from Spiegel—or from any catalog company—wasn't what we expected. It was: How can they return a catalog purchase if they don't like a product after it's delivered?

We responded to that concern by running ads where we stressed the simplicity of returning a purchase.

The ads worked. Suddenly, our advertising was right on the mark.

We also avoided making a common advertising mistake: letting the product dominate. Unless you have a unique, terrific product or a stranglehold on the market, don't overestimate your product's worth—or, more to the point, your customers' need to know what makes your product tick.

In most cases, your audience will understand your product's function and benefits. That's why more and more advertisers are going away from the old saw about making the product the star. How many beer commercials have you seen recently that emphasize the product's taste? How many car commercials that dwell on the auto's features? Instead of the product, the ads focus on such things as life-style and service. Customers are better informed than ever before, and if you repeat what they already know, you'll lose them.

Use your common sense. Advertising is a method of communication, and it provides advertisers with a great opportunity to provide customers with important information. Don't blow it!

Let's say you have a lawn service. What should your ads say? What do people who contact a lawn service really want to know? I'll tell you this. If someone were to run an ad that guaranteed they'd be at a house exactly when they promised or they'd cut the lawn for free, they'd have more business than they knew what to do with. Nothing burns up a homeowner more than waiting around for the lawn cutters to arrive and they show up hours or even days late. Address customers' primary concerns and they'll love you for it.

Take a look at ads in the Yellow Pages. I'd estimate the majority of those ads say the wrong things. Pick out a category: typewriter repairs, for instance. How many ads communicate the average length of time for service? Am I going to be without my typewriter for a day, a week or a month? Next, see how many list the brands of typewriters they repair. Those two pieces of information are absolutely essential for prospective customers, yet they're frequently ignored.

Target, personalize, segment, niche market. The days of throwing a national ad out to everyone are gone. Specialized selling is essential. You have to find your customer, and you can't do it without considering these factors: demographics, income, life-style, age, significance of geography, relative cost of product. The narrower you can define your market, the better chance you'll have of successfully marketing to it.

Finally, use your advertising to communicate your dream. It is your most valuable resource. If the corporate dream is on the mark—if it is the right idea at the right time—it has enormous, intrinsic selling power. Use it!

From the graphics to the words, your advertising should do more than simply sell a product or service. It should capture your dream and communicate it convincingly. This isn't just the job of institutional advertising—the traditional corporate identity campaign. Customers should be able to find the dream in your advertising slogan, in the logo, in the headline, in the design of a mailing piece. The vision that drives your company shouldn't take a back seat in your advertising.

It's not a matter of spelling out your dream every time you run your ads. It's more a question of style, tone and philosophy. At Spiegel, our ads and mailing pieces reflected what we were trying to become: a fine department store in print. Using everything from high-quality paper stock to the distinctive new Spiegel logo, we communicated our dream.

Internal Marketing

Whether consciously or unconsciously, many companies separate themselves from their customers in their marketing strategies. It's true for companies who make catalogs and for companies who sell electricity. If the personality and philosophy of your company is different from that of your customers, your marketing won't work.

If, for instance, you have an elitist corporate culture and your marketing is designed to appeal to the common man, there's a big gap. If you've targeted an upscale group and your employees aren't aware of all the ramifications of the word, you can't achieve your marketing goals.

Look at stores that emphasize service, that tell the customer in ads that they bend over backwards to meet their needs. But when you walk into a store looking for a product, the sales clerk says, ''I can't answer your question; I just work the cash register,'' or ''Hey, if it's not on the rack, we don't have it.'' The problem, of course, is that the company hasn't made an effort to get its employees thinking like its customers.

At Spiegel, my refrain was: ''What you do and what you say,

every day and every way, says something about your company.''
When you walk into a hotel, you immediately form an impression
based on how you're greeted, how quickly and smoothly you
check in, by how the lobby looks.

It doesn't take much more than a long line at the registration
desk for even the most loyal customers to fall out of love.

The companies that have voice mail systems are great examples of organizations that have separated themselves from their
customers. In almost every case, they've implemented voice mail
for the company's convenience, not the customers. I can't imagine a worse marketing approach in this age of personalization
than having a machine answer the phone. Adding insult to injury,
the machine is equipped with so many response options that the
answer to your question is delayed ad infinitum. This is also an
age where speedy service is prized, so voice mail commits yet
another marketing sin.

I am convinced that voice mail won't nurture a customer's love
for a company.

It all begins with a corporate-wide commitment to customers.
Think about when you went to a doctor's office for an appoint-
ment. You arrived on time, but you were forced to sit an hour in a
crowded waiting room because the doctor was more concerned
about his schedule than yours. The doctor failed to live up to his
commitment, as do many companies. You have to be obsessed
about your commitments.

Supermarkets have made a commitment to cut down on the
waiting time in lines. They've done so with scanners, a significant expense that more than pays for itself in customer satisfaction.

Hotels and restaurants have done it with nonsmoking sections.
They've recognized that a majority of their patrons don't want to
breathe smoke while eating an expensive meal or sleep in rooms
with the lingering smell of tobacco.

Customers love companies who live up to their commitments.

Marketing a Mystique

Some companies enjoy a wonderful reputation and image. As soon as someone says the company's name, your reaction is positive. They have an aura about them, an almost magical mystique.

They achieve that aura through marketing. It's not just a few corporate identity campaigns that help them reach this plateau. It's the sum-total of hundreds of little things, dictated by a single-minded belief in the corporate dream.

A good marketer treats everyone alike. You can't treat your customers with kindness and your suppliers with disdain and expect the marketing equation to work. In other words, you can't be two-faced. I'm sure you know of companies that advertise their fairness and honesty, and then squeeze their resources for every penny they can get, showing little loyalty and less concern for their problems. That will come back to haunt both a company and its customers. Squeeze a resource too hard and he'll sneak in higher prices or skimp on quality. Ultimately, your customer will suffer the consequences. As the saying goes, what goes around comes around.

Marketing isn't solely the job of the marketing department. Everyone in an organization has a role to play.

How do you get everyone to play it? There is a word that has become popular in relation to building contacts: networking. Every company has its own network of employees, suppliers, media and customers. Your daily interaction with each person in that network is crucial. If your network is operating on the same wavelength, something wonderful will happen. Your company will have an aura, a mystique. Suddenly, your marketing will work.

Start internally. Communicate your company's dream and let your people use their initiative to carry it out. When your people believe in and understand the goal, they'll be able to contribute to the marketing effort. Someone in your traffic department will be faced with a routing option: either saving the company a dollar through a less-expensive delivery service or getting the product to the customer a day earlier. The traffic manager, if he understands the company's goal, won't choose to save the company a dollar at the expense of the customer. He'll recognize that the customer doesn't care if the company saves a dollar; that his job is to get the customer a product as fast as possible. Similarly, if someone in the packaging department sees that a new packaging method results in boxes becoming dirty or unattractive, she'll automatically respond to the unattractive package by finding a better way.

Every oral or written communication—whether to employees or nonemployees—is a small but important part of your marketing. Don't overlook even the most mundane messages. A bill to a customer says a lot about your company. If it's hard to read or cheap-looking or the customer's name is spelled wrong, it will reflect negatively.

Finally, be prepared for the inevitable economic downturn. At some point, your company will have to tighten its belt. This is when your marketing is most vulnerable; this is when customers fall out of love with companies. During tough economic times, organizations often cut service expenses. They reduce their customer service staffs, shorten their hours or eliminate a toll-free number.

My advice: Don't! In fact, the wise corporation will spend even more on service during economic downturns. While your competitors are cutting back, you should increase your expenditures on things customers love. Though it might make it tough in the short term, in the long run you'll emerge much better off.

Get the Message Out in a Hundred Ways

Don't be shy or inconsistent in selling your company's dream. The more tactics you use, the better. Don't limit yourself to the traditional tactics: advertising, direct marketing, public relations, sales promotion.

Phone calls, letters, meetings, conferences, one-on-one conversations, packaging, presentations, logos—your communication resources are huge. Maximize their effectiveness not only by using them, but by using them to drum home a consistent message.

It requires coordination. You have to coordinate the efforts of your people as well as your outside marketing services agencies. Determine what needs to be said and make sure everyone is saying it as forcefully and convincingly as possible.

At Spiegel, we wanted to communicate that buying from Spiegel was chic. We wanted to eliminate the notion that buying from our catalog—from any catalog—was something only less affluent people did. We needed to demonstrate that if you were an affluent, working woman, you didn't have to hide our catalog.

We had to market our chic. When someone picked up our catalog, we wanted them to perceive the book as stylish and trendy. When a resource visited our offices, we wanted them to leave with the impression of a hot, aggressive company. When the media conducted an interview with one of our executives, we wanted the reporter convinced she was writing about someone who had his finger on the pulse of the fashion world. When a customer called our toll-free number, we needed our representative to impress the caller with her courtesy, knowledge and state-of-the-art ordering system.

Once the dream was in place and communicated throughout the company, it wasn't hard to synchronize our message to the outside world. Even though there were thousands of employees sending hundreds of thousands of messages, they were all saying the same thing in different ways: Spiegel is the chic place to shop.

You Can't Buy Love

An enormous budget for successful marketing isn't necessary. Money is helpful in spreading the word about your company and its products or services, but many of the country's largest corporations have been fighting increasing customer disloyalty.

Money can't buy love.

Think about the products and establishments you love. Perhaps it's Reebok athletic shoes. Or Honda cars. Or the little bookstore around the corner that always has the titles you're looking for and a pleasant environment for browsing.

These organizations have two things in common: they don't overemphasize the product side of the business to the detriment of the service side; they have developed a vision of their business and everyone in the organization understands and is working toward that vision.

When you strip marketing of all its academic theories and fancy applications, you're left with the goal of making the customer love you. It is an achievable goal for companies of every size and type.

Starting with the CEO and working down to the mailroom clerk, all employees must make that goal a priority. If that happens, great marketing will follow.

CHAPTER EIGHTEEN

Organizing for Change

Dream strategies demand that companies respond to change quickly and easily. They require flexibility and adaptability. They place a premium on clear, concise internal communication.

The traditional pyramid structure of American corporations, though, is ill suited to implementing dream strategies. Pyramid organizations are similar to lumbering battleships, unable to change course without expending a great deal of effort and energy.

The flat line organization, on the other hand, is like a sleek, well-designed motorboat, easy to maneuver and able to change speeds instantly. For corporate dreamers, it is the ideal vehicle to get you where you want to go.

The Upward Push

Who is in the best position to take responsibility and account-ability for decisions? When a new computer system is being contemplated, who should choose it? The executive vice president or the manager of information services (MIS)?

In pyramid organizations, the decision is inevitably made by the executive vice president. The MIS guy, who because of his knowledge, experience and daily work is in the best position to make the decision, is not allowed to do so.

Pyramids push decision-making upward. They remove responsibility and accountability from lower-level managers. The bureaucratic upper-crust—all the executive, senior and just plain vice presidents—usurp the functions that logically should fall a level or two beneath them.

Traditional Distortion

The multiple layers of a pyramid organization distort communication.

Why? Because the more layers an idea passes through, the more interpretation it receives. It's similar to the children's game of "telephone," where one kid says a sentence and whispers it to another child, who in turn whispers the sentence to a third child, until the message is communicated around the group. The last child then says the sentence out loud, and it is always hopelessly garbled.

Everyone wants to put his spin on the original idea. The COO (Chief Operating Officer) slightly alters the CEO's directive; a division president shades the concept with his bias; a staff executive vice president adds his input.

As they do so, you can imagine their comments: "The idea's good, but it's never going to fly in my department. We're going to have to do a little differently." Or "Well, maybe if we cut the expenditures a bit and change the focus, we might be able to make it work."

The only way a CEO in this kind of organization can ensure that his program is implemented exactly as he conceived it is to accompany his directive with a threat: Anyone failing to comply will face serious consequences. Of course, such a threat undermines the idea. Managers will respond without enthusiasm, grumbling and dragging their feet as they implement the new program.

The Flat Line Concept

Flat line management calls for the elimination of extraneous titles at the top. Pyramid organizations are top-heavy with vice chairmen, chief operating officers, presidents, executive vice presidents, senior vice presidents.

Clear the decks. Begin with the CEO at the top, and a limited number of vice presidents reporting directly to him (or her). The number of vice presidents should be limited by an organization's specialized areas—operations, finance, marketing and so on. Underneath the vice presidents are the managers of each division.

Next, delegate! Unlike a pyramid-style organization, decision-making should be pushed down to the implementer level; the person who is in the best position to make a given decision should have the responsibility and accountability to do so.

Third, push decisions down quickly. Don't let a decision bounce around among vice presidents and the CEO. Speed is essential, and a flat line organization is built for speed.

The Flat Line CEO

Many CEOs have only a few people reporting directly to them. A flat line structure demands far more. At Spiegel, for instance, I had eight vice presidents who reported directly to me.

If that seems to be an overwhelming number, remember that a flat line structure depends on delegating responsibility and accountability. That means the CEO delegates as well as his vice presidents.

A CEO should be responsible for no more than 10 percent of a company's decisions.

That percentage might shock some people. With such a small amount of decision-making power, how does a CEO control an organization's strategy?

By communicating his vision to everyone, starting with his vice presidents. It is not simply a matter of saying, ''This is my dream.'' It involves constant communication, explanation, analysis, monitoring.

More than once, my people came up to me and said, ''Mr. Johnson, sometimes we just don't get it.'' So I would do everything within my power to try and help them ''get it.'' That took time, but time is on the side of a CEO running a flat line organization. People weren't always running to me asking for decisions; I wasn't the one who was going to decide whether we should choose one supplier over another. The merchandising manager was empowered to make that decision.

I spent my time working out strategy with my managers, discussing the parameters of the changes we were attempting, going back and forth over the issues. We concentrated on three points: 1. An overview of long-terms goals. 2. The starting points to achieve those goals. 3. The priority of different steps toward those goals over time.

Once I felt they understood these three points, I gave them room to run. I rarely saddled them with paperwork designed to document their progress. How were they going to move forward if they were stuck filling out forms and reports? Though I might have occasionally asked for written notes, most of the follow-up was verbal. Usually, I'd end our meetings by saying, ''How about if you come back in sixty days and we'll get together and see how you and your team are doing?''

Usually, they would be doing very well. The flat line structure encouraged leadership on all levels. It provided managers with more authority than they had ever had in their corporate lives. Most people respond positively to that authority. When managers aren't hamstrung by a bureaucracy and someone continually looking over their shoulder, their leadership qualities emerge. When they aren't intimidated by layers of upper-level managers poised to usurp their authority, they go about their jobs with unusual diligence and enthusiasm.

Roadblocks to Flat Line Management

If a flat line structure makes so much sense, why do so many organizations cling to the pyramid? They do so for four reasons.

First, tradition. Whether it comes from academia or elsewhere, the pyramid is the accepted way of structuring large organizations. There are rules: anything higher than a four-to-one reporting ratio is bad. There is a false comfort in this organizational tradition, but it still has an undeniable attractiveness for many CEOs.

Second, authority. The pyramid has more titles to pass around than a flat line structure. It permits a company to offer fancy titles as rewards, dangling authoritative-sounding positions such as division president or executive vice president in front of power-hungry corporate climbers.

Third, ego. CEOs and other top executives frequently isolate themselves from the commoners. They enjoy the inherent class divisions of the pyramid structure. A certain type of CEO relishes having scores of vice presidents arranged beneath him in an intricate pecking order. He's the type of chief executive who says, "Screen my calls" and "Let somebody else handle that." His ego demands the pyramid.

Fourth, laziness. The pyramid is a crutch. Some executives worry that without it they'll flounder. To a certain extent, that's true. A flat line organization demands well-thought-out and clearly communicated goals. It requires planning and conceptual thinking.

But it doesn't require spending every waking hour in the office. I've read surveys that show the average executive work week to be sixty hours. I don't think it does anyone any good to be chained to the office. The pyramid structure, unfortunately, encourages excessive hours. Top executives are inundated by details, by unending minor decisions that place unreasonable demands on their time.

A flat line organization, executed properly, can literally run by itself. At Spiegel, I made a deal with my people. I told them: Don't call me at home and I'll never call you when I'm away.

I stuck to that deal, as did my people. You might think that impossible. After all, Spiegel was an organization undergoing tremendous changes. Decisions on new products, people, policies and services were made every day.

Yet I didn't have to make the majority of those decisions. The system worked. I didn't take work home and I didn't work on weekends. Most of my executives followed suit. If someone didn't take a vacation because they were too busy, I didn't give him brownie points for his dedication. In fact, I chastised him for not delegating properly.

People need time off to recharge their batteries, and if you're working round the clock, you're a good candidate for burnout.

Therefore, if you're an overworked CEO who can't find time for anything beyond the details, think about a flat line system as a way to escape your chains. Imagine what it would be like to sit in your office and have the time to work on the big picture. If that's not a strong incentive for flat line management, nothing is.

Do You Need Permission?

"I'd like to get your permission before I start on this project."

How many times has a subordinate asked his boss this question? Far too many. When someone would ask it of me, I'd respond, "Why do you need my permission?"

I tried to show my people that they didn't need my permission. What they needed was a belief in themselves. When people ask for permission, they are asking for another person to take responsibility. Companies that are built on permission-asking hierarchies are asking for trouble.

That doesn't mean a lower-level executive can authorize a multimillion-dollar expenditure without consulting higher-level managers. I'm talking about permission in a broader sense. I'm referring to a mind-set. One of the most familiar phrases in corporate America is, "I'd like to run this by you." Translated, that means, "I have this idea, but if it bombs, I don't want you to say that I didn't warn you first."

Corporate managers need the freedom to fail. Failure isn't good. But many companies are organized around the principle of failure-avoidance. Employees are afraid to take risks because the corporate culture systematically punishes failure. But all managerial levels should be encouraged to take chances. The culture and the CEO should make risk-taking a requirement of the job.

At Spiegel, people would come into my office and I'd ask them how a project was going. When could we implement the plan?

"I'm not sure," they'd reply. "I'm not sure whether it's right?"

"What do you mean? Are you at least 10 percent sure it will work?"

"Oh, more than that," they'd say.

"Well, how about 100 percent?"

"No, I'm not that sure. Maybe 70 percent."

"Okay," I'd say. "Don't you think 70 percent is enough? We've got to make changes. If we wait until we get to 95 percent sure, we'll never make those changes. How much more time do you need until you're 80 percent sure it will work?"

"I don't really know."

"But how do you feel about it now? Should we abandon the idea? Or is it worth pursuing?"

"Oh, yes," they'd say, "I really think we ought to do it."

"Then do it!"

I pushed my people to make decisions and take responsibility for their decisions. It was the only way we would move forward. Unlike some companies, Spiegel wasn't structured to reward those who made the fewest mistakes. Those who became stars took chances; they pushed their ideas even though those ideas might not pan out.

Gradually, everyone at Spiegel understood that the company wasn't a classroom, that they didn't have to raise their hands to get permission. As adults, they were empowered to act on their own, as long they acted in accordance with the company's goals.

Keep It Simple

Corporations suffer from clutter. Contributing to that clutter are bureaucratic red tape, mandatory reports, memos and other paperwork, committees and meetings. Though it's difficult to eliminate the clutter entirely—especially in large organizations—it can be minimized.

First, limit the number of approvals necessary before implementation. For most projects, it's unnecessary for five or ten top executives to sign off before the implementer gets the okay. Ask yourself what one person is in the best position to approve a project. That's the one approval that's necessary.

Second, avoid decisions by committee. You don't want your organization to mirror the decision-making process of the United States Congress. A bill is introduced, and it has great promise and purpose. Over time, however, it gets watered down. Special interest groups effectively lobby senators, and it gets locked up in committee. The only way to get it out of committee is by tacking on provision after provision. When the bill finally passes and becomes law, it is a pale version of its former self, vastly inferior.

Don't let that happen in your organization. Don't allow every vice president to add his two cents if a project is outside his area of expertise. Give the project's creator control and maintain the project's integrity.

Third, avoid paperwork. Too often, lengthy reports are just another form of asking permission. They're used to justify an idea. They analyze ideas to death, raising all possibilities and creating "what if" scenarios.

You don't need all that. When we decided to go after higher quality sources at Spiegel, we didn't create hundreds of pages of research about each source. We simply drew up a list of brands carried by fine department stores and went after them. We used our common sense to break things down into manageable elements.

Get the Right People

What sort of executives fit best in a flat line organization?

Though there isn't one specific type, you should look for certain characteristics. Obviously, they need the proper technical and managerial expertise. But beyond that, they need the capacity to believe in a dream.

Cynics, naysayers and risk-avoiders aren't acceptable. When I started bringing in people to Spiegel, I always told them about my dream for the company and gauged their reactions. I didn't expect any of them to scoff; no one in his right mind would do so in a job interview with a CEO. But at the very least, I wanted people to give the dream the benefit of the doubt. They didn't have to say they loved it. As long as they were enthusiastic about its possibilities, they would fit into the new Spiegel.

I also looked for good communicators. In a flat line organization, you need vice presidents who can clearly and inspirationally convey the company's vision to subordinates. I hired five new vice presidents, all with varying levels of communication skills. Though some of them were more advanced than others in this area, they were all willing to improve those skills. Communication techniques can be taught, and after a few years, all our vice presidents were selling our dream convincingly and motivationally.

Finally, you need decision-makers. After a while, my vice presidents could anticipate the first question out of my mouth: What decisions have you made lately? Usually, they had the right answers. A flat line organization can't afford buck-passers and devil's advocates at the top.

A Structure That Works for All

Flat line management works for all organizations—big and small, public and private, those in turnaround situations and those that are market leaders.

A flat line organization's best attribute is that it facilitates change. In today's and tomorrow's environment, change is unavoidable. Whether you're Proctor & Gamble or a small local company, you will be forced to adapt to new economic, social and industry trends.

Without a flat line structure, change is difficult. A pyramid-style company trying to revamp its products or services will face a steep, uphill climb. The changes a CEO demands will be distorted as they slowly, arduously filter down through the bureaucratic layers. The middle-level managers who should be responsible for making those changes will be denied the opportunity to do so.

A flat line organization, on the other hand, can respond swiftly and easily. The CEO's message of change will flash through the company, free of interpretation or bias. Department heads will be ready and able to translate strategy into action.

Until such time as the pace of change slows, more and more companies will realize that flat line management is the only structure that makes sense.

CHAPTER NINETEEN

Crisis Management

Much has been written about crisis management. Unfortunately, little of it is relevant to most companies.

Crises of the magnitude of a criminal's tampering with Tylenol packages or an Exxon oil spill are rare. It's fine to prepare yourself for that possibility, but such contingency plans generally are never implemented.

It is a mistake to prepare only for major crises, especially if you're a company embarking on a dream strategy. If your vision is innovative, daring and new (which it should be), you'll encounter all manner of difficulties. From the conception to the inception stage, the dream's bugs have to be worked out. During the workout stage—which can last years—you'll stumble upon unexpected obstacles. This is something every dream strategist should prepare for. Unlike reheated strategies, your new blend of ideas will take some getting used to; you're going to have to tinker, to fashion solutions to inevitable problems.

These problems—or what I like to refer to as minor crises—will occur regularly, and if you're unprepared for them, their effect is anything but minor.

Let's look at a recent example of a company facing an emergency situation.

The Lexus Scenario

When the Toyota Motor Company introduced their Lexus luxury car, they learned of defects in the cruise control and brake light systems. They reacted with an immediate recall of the 9,000 cars sold. They also publicized the recall and asked their dealers personally to call people to whom they had sold a Lexus and explain the recall.

Typically, car companies do everything possible to minimize word of a recall. Sometimes, they do nothing more than instruct their dealers to only respond to customer complaints; to let the customer take the initiative when and if they discover a problem. At best, they try to soft-pedal the recall, refusing to talk to the media and issuing impersonal letters to owners of a recalled car.

Toyota reacted with speed, honesty and concern. No one forced them to react in that manner. It certainly must have been difficult for them to act as they did given the importance of the Lexus introduction and the fact that it was positioned as a high-quality automobile.

Did they overreact? Not at all. Toyota brought a crisis management mentality to a situation others might have viewed only as a problem. They had a dream of a startlingly new luxury car, and they moved quickly and convincingly to solve a crisis that threatened the dream.

Spiegel's Crisis

In an earlier chapter, I related what happened when Spiegel attempted to convert to a state-of-the-art computer warehousing system; how we lost control of our inventory, 65,000 stockkeeping units spread among six warehouses; how we couldn't find products customers ordered, resulting in lengthy shipping delays and millions of dollars in losses.

Was this a major crisis? Not really. Though it was a serious problem for the company and our customers, its impact was limited and there was no controversy or social issue involved. But we treated it as if the lives of millions would be affected by our decisions. And in a sense, that was the case. Millions of customers wouldn't receive their orders when they expected.

We had a number of options. We could have junked our new computer system and gone back to the old one. We could have increased our back orders and maintained a business-as-usual facade, hoping that our customers would tolerate the delays. We could have offered excuses, blaming computer technology and telling our customers it wasn't really our fault.

We did none of those things. The first option would have meant relying on an outmoded, manual warehousing system that would cause untold problems for customers in the future. Though it might have temporarily helped the situation, the long-term consequences would have been awful.

The second option would have meant a cover-up. It would have broken the bond of trust we had with our customers.

The third option would have meant scapegoating our technology. As I've stated before, customers don't care about your excuses.

We chose to inform our customers immediately about our computer breakdown. By way of phone and letter, we apologized for the inconvenience and said that if they were disappointed, we hoped they would give us a second chance. We also spared no expense in our efforts. Not only did we pour money into ridding our computer system of bugs, but we took extraordinary measures to reorder products from sources. In many instances, we would order duplicates to replace those lost in the warehouse, flying them in so that customers would receive products faster.

We survived. In fact, we immediately shot back up to the $25 million profit level the next year when our computer system was working.

You probably see the parallels between our approach to the crisis and Toyota's. Speed, honesty, and concern for customers governed our actions. In addition, we refused to let cost dictate our response. Both Toyota and Spiegel treated problems as crises.

What helped Spiegel most of all during this crisis was our dream. We resolved to take no action that would be at odds with our vision of the company; we refused to let the crisis force us into a decision that would betray the dream.

I knew that our dream would bring profits back to pre-computer levels. We had labored long and hard to build a new Spiegel, and customers had responded. As long as we preserved Spiegel's philosophy, we would rebound from our setback. The crisis was a surface storm, and the dream was deep-rooted. By keeping the dream healthy, our future growth was assured.

Customer Reaction

One of the easiest traps to fall into when a problem or emergency occurs is underestimating customers' concerns. It is true that customers will forgive companies that respond appropriately to crises. But the wrong response will engender a long and strong outcry. More often than not, this is why small crises are mishandled.

You might recall what happened recently when Kraft ran a promotion and because of a printing error, thousands of people mistakenly thought they had won vans. Kraft announced that an error had been made and that the vast majority of people would not be getting vans. To assuage those people, Kraft offered a small amount of money. But it wasn't enough. The media publicized consumers' outrage and disappointment, interviewing scores of people who railed against Kraft and threatened lawsuits.

Perhaps Kraft executives felt that people would understand that mistakes happen, that they would realize Kraft's intention was not to give away thousands of vans. Unfortunately, Kraft wasn't looking at the problem from the perspective of the customer. They weren't putting themselves in the shoes of someone who had leaped high into the air upon discovering that she had won a $15,000 van.

Ultimately, Kraft did realize the extent of consumers' negative reaction and significantly increased the compensation. But they should have offered the larger amount immediately.

In a crisis, don't try to "move up" to the solution. When you up the ante later on, you're viewed as indecisive; you're viewed as being somewhat less than sincere.

To avoid this situation, make your resolution of a crisis swift and permanent. Don't backtrack or second-guess yourself. Nothing you do days or weeks after the crisis will have as much impact as what you do initially.

Spare No Cost

Crisis resolution costs money. However, different forms of resolution cost different amounts. In many companies, someone (often the financial V.P.) will suggest that there be a budget for crisis resolution tactics, that one course of action is preferable to another because it requires less money.

Don't bow to financial considerations! Cost should be irrelevant when crises occur. Certainly you don't want to overspend. But if you allow your actions to be dictated by costs, you're likely to make a serious blunder.

Toyota rightly ignored cost considerations in their approach to the Lexus crisis. Kraft took a different approach when they initially tried to limit their monetary loss.

Your most valuable asset is customer relationships. Is it worth saving $100,000 and risking damage to that relationship? $1 million? I think it is hard to find a dollar amount that justifies the risk if you approach it from a long-term perspective.

Consider the Emotional Issue

Don't overlook the emotional component of a crisis; it's not just what the customer thinks of you, it's what she feels about you. Remember, a dream strategy is an emotion-laden one. More so than a dreamless organization, your success is tied to creating new feelings about your company in the hearts and minds of your customers. Consider the issues that might have a negative impact on your market's feelings.

When the Cabbage Patch Doll craze hit, we found ourselves deluged with orders—over 50,000 of them. Like everyone else, our supply couldn't keep up with the demand. Our customers were ordering the dolls with the hope that they would arrive at their homes before Christmas. We knew that was impossible.

We had a number of ways to deal with this problem. We could have simply told our customers that they should look for the dolls elsewhere. Or we could have taken their money when they ordered and explained that there would be a delay in shipping.

But either alternative would have avoided the emotional aspect of the crisis. People did not look at Cabbage Patch Dolls as just another product. Telling them to look elsewhere would result in intense disappointment in Spiegel: we would be failing to deliver what our catalog promised. If we took their money and delayed sending them their product, they would feel both disappointed and cheated.

We decided on a third alternative. We straightforwardly told our customers we were placing the dolls on back order and that we would be able to ship them in January. We acknowledged our difficulty in securing the product and explained that we would take their orders now but not charge them. When we had our 50,000 dolls in stock, we would contact them and give them the opportunity to confirm their orders and pay for the dolls.

Certainly some of our customers were disappointed that we couldn't fill their orders before Christmas. But we also avoided greater disappointment by quickly and honestly informing them of the situation. We ended up shipping 35,000 dolls in January to customers who chose to wait rather than risk not finding the dolls in stock elsewhere.

If you don't attempt to control the fiery emotions engendered by a crisis, they can quickly spread. By addressing the potential for disappointment among our customers, we contained the blaze.

Don't Be Afraid to Sound the Alarm

It's easy to take a noncrisis approach to problems. You ignore or give scant attention to something that will have minimal, immediate impact on the company.

Though you don't want to bring all your resources to bear on a relatively small matter, it's equally dangerous to underreact. By taking small problems seriously, you increase the odds that they won't become big problems.

At Spiegel we called it "sounding the alarm." When a problem developed, I encouraged my people to ring the bell so everyone could hear it. For instance, we had a women's shoe that was selling very well. Then we received a customer call complaining that one of the nails in the shoe was poking through the heel.

Normally, customer complaints are written up and passed through channels, and an inspection is conducted and a conclusion reached about the problem. The process could take weeks.

When the alarm rang, however, the process was greatly accelerated. We immediately stopped shipping the shoe and inspected it for the defect. We wrote all the customers who had purchased the shoe and informed them about the problem, asking them to inspect their shoes and determine if they saw a nail protruding.

In and of itself, the shoe defect wasn't a big thing. But look at it within a larger context. There are hundreds of problems like this that occur in a given year. What happens if you don't sound

195

the alarm for any of them? What if you procrastinate? What if you don't take the problems seriously?

There's a domino effect. Instead of fifty dissatisfied customers, you have five thousand. Customers begin talking to each other and sharing their negative experiences. Perhaps the bad word-of-mouth tips the media that something is wrong, and negative stories are written. Ultimately, your image is damaged.

Remember: It is far better to tell your customers about a problem than have them tell you about it. It makes a big difference in their perception of your organization. If you assign the customer a higher priority than yourself, you'll reap the benefits.

Crisis Prevention

No company can eliminate all problems, emergencies and major crises. But an organization can prepare for them, reducing the number and limiting the damage.

How do you prepare?

First, by trying to be perfect. Notice that I didn't say, "being perfect." Perfection is impossible. But you should attempt to come as close as possible.

Many organizations have an acceptable margin for error. But what's acceptable? Ten percent? Fifteen percent? The higher the margin for error, the greater the likelihood that mistakes will be made—mistakes that lead to problems. So why not aim for perfection? If you make that your target, you will make fewer mistakes than if you take a "nobody's perfect" attitude.

A philosophy of perfection is a crucial part of a crisis prevention strategy. The more employees you have striving for perfection, the fewer problems your organization will encounter.

Second, treat small problems as if they were big ones. Perhaps nine times out of ten, those little, irritating snafus won't turn into anything. But it is that tenth one that will kill you. You're not going to know which problem is going to explode, so you have to handle all of them with extreme care.

Recently, I boarded an airplane, and when they closed the door before takeoff, the closed-door indicator light failed to go on. Because I was seated in the first row, I could hear the conversation between the captain and his crew members about the situation. The captain said the door seemed to be securely latched, but he wasn't absolutely sure; it was a new plane, and he wasn't familiar with the electrical system. He decided to delay takeoff and make sure there was nothing wrong.

We were three hours late arriving at our destination. They announced that there would be people at the service desk to help people make connections and rooms reserved for those who missed connections.

I and the other passengers weren't happy with the late arrival. But the captain's actions helped the small problem remain small. If the door had swung open 30,000 feet up in the air, it would have been a bigger problem.

The captain put safety first. He offered no excuses, though he could easily have blamed the new plane Boeing sent the airline. He was willing to create a minor inconvenience to avoid a major problem.

Third, never underestimate customers' capacity to forgive. Too often, companies believe that their customers won't tolerate mistakes, that they'll hold a grudge against a company for years.

I don't believe that is true. Americans are the most forgiving people on earth. But a company has to earn its customers' forgiveness. You earn it by playing straight with them, by acting quickly and decisively. Certainly, they'll respond negatively if you blunder, as in the case of Kraft's van promotion. But customers are as quick to forgive as they are to anger. Give them a chance to do so.

The CEO's Role

When a major crisis hits, the CEO almost automatically takes charge. The seriousness of the situation demands his leadership.

But the CEO should not neglect the smaller crises—the commonplace problems and emergencies—that plague every company. It is his (or her) job to step forward and take control. The CEO who delegates this responsibility to a subordinate is delegating away an assignment that is naturally his.

By being responsible and accountable for minor crises, the CEO demonstrates to everyone—both inside and outside the organization—that he takes the situation seriously. He is communicating to customers his concern and to employees that they should make the crisis a high priority.

In addition, CEOs can see the big picture best in a crisis. They are the ones who won't lose sight of the company's driving vision. When CEOs manage crises, they should refuse to bow to short-term solutions that threaten to dilute the company's vision.

It is not that others in the company aren't capable of handling a problem or emergency. It is simply that chief executives, because of their authority and vision, are in the best position to lead organizations through the crisis.

CHAPTER TWENTY

Turnarounds

What is a turnaround? Taken literally, it means changing an organization's direction. It implies a dramatic change in a company's substance and style, resulting in a better, healthier company.

Turnarounds don't take place without someone or something pushing it. No magical financial wand can be waved to make it happen.

Turnarounds are generated by repositioning, by taking a company that has been operating one way and making it operate another way. It might not be a total repositioning; changing only one or two aspects of the organization might be all that's needed.

What does the repositioning process involve and where does it start? Typically, companies recognize the need for change in response to financial troubles. They decide something major has to be done to cure the organization's financial woes.

But you shouldn't wait until the situation becomes desperate. Far better if you anticipate serious problems rather than react to them.

What's Going On Out There?

Company A is in trouble. Competitive pressures from imports combined with falling market share in a few key product lines has resulted in declining profits in recent quarters. But Company A thinks it sees the light at the end of the tunnel. Their R&D people have come up with a terrific technology that will enable them to create a new product superior to anything on the market.

This is a typical example of a company trying to turn itself around from the inside rather than the outside. They've failed to monitor and analyze what's taking place in the outside world, assuming that if they create a better mousetrap, the world will beat a path to their door.

Though that may happen, it is a very difficult way to produce a turnaround. A far easier way is for companies to keep their eyes glued on outside forces. At least once a year, organizations should take in-depth looks at all the forces that affect their market.

Is the market changing? Is it receding, failing, becoming mature? Why? Are there more or fewer companies serving the market than the previous year? How are new technologies affecting the market? What about life-style changes? Cultural changes? Ecological changes?

It is a big world out there, and something is happening that could be the key to a successful repositioning strategy. You don't have to be a futurist to take advantage of change. You merely have to be keenly observant and analytical. Create "what if" scenarios. What if that new synthetic material the Japanese are working on becomes reality? What if electromagnetic fields are found to be injurious to people's health? What if domestic labor costs continue to skyrocket and foreign labor costs remain stable? What if the downturn in your industry continues and even worsens, and there's no upturn in sight?

Don't rest your repositioning hopes only on what you know and what you've done; that limits your opportunities. Explore what's taking place outside your small, insular environment.

Act Early

The longer you wait to act, the harder it will be to reposition yourself successfully. Many troubled companies have a tendency to dig in and try to weather the bombardment. They're like infantry in foxholes, praying for the bombs to stop falling. Unfortunately, if you wait too long, the destruction around you will be such that there won't be much left when you emerge from your hole.

You'll probably recall a company called Sperry & Hutchison, creators of S&H green stamps. In the fifties and early sixties, it seemed like everyone collected those green stamps from stores, painstakingly pasting them into books and exchanging the books for a variety of products.

When times began to change, S&H ignored the early warning signs. The proliferation of sale prices and discounters gradually eroded retailers' and consumers' motivations for giving and collecting green stamps. In addition, significant changes in society—such as the use of credit cards instead of cash—made it more difficult for green stamps to be distributed. Finally, the concept behind green stamps gradually became old-fashioned— can you imagine today's busy, working woman taking the time to paste all those stamps in a little book?

But S&H didn't notice until it was too late. Perhaps if they had, they could have repositioned their product to take advantage of the shifting marketplace.

Some companies would rather deny the harsh realities than accept them. Who wants to be the first to say that a product line will soon be outmoded or a distribution will become inefficient? You risk the wrath of stockholders, superiors, boards of directors. Far better to close your eyes and make a wish that things will get better.

They won't. Every passing week will make things worse.

Jump on the first sign of change. Study it. Discuss it with other executives. Do research to confirm the signs. Then prepare a response. As long as you don't wait too long, there's a good chance for successful repositioning.

Moderate or Radical Repositioning?

At Spiegel, we changed everything. We did so not because we wanted to, but because we had to. The situation was so bad that anything less than a radical repositioning would have been useless.

Most companies won't find themselves in this situation; they will not have let things deteriorate to the point that only massive, corporate-wide change is required.

It is far more likely that a company will have to reposition one aspect of itself: a product line, sales division or distribution method. Whatever it is, it must be taken apart and put back together in a significantly different way, attuned to a given change in the outside world.

If your cost of selling has become unacceptably high because of changes in demographics or buying habits of your customers, you might have to switch from a sales force to telemarketing.

If your market segment has aged and a new generation is looking to competitors for a particular product, you might have to scrap the old line and introduce a new one more in keeping with your targeted segment.

Don't be afraid to hone in on the problem and take whatever measures are necessary to solve it. Superficial or half-hearted repositioning won't work! You must go all the way, even if it means violating corporate tradition and overcoming the objections of the more conservative members of your staff.

Think Beyond the Financials

Don't confuse repositioning and turnarounds with financial restructuring. Organizations with serious problems frequently respond by downsizing, selling off unprofitable divisions and generally "trimming the fat." The result is a nice-looking balance sheet.

But it is not a turnaround. In the vast majority of cases, the problems that brought a company to such dire straits are outside, not inside. No amount of cost-cutting can affect those outside forces. Financial measures provide only temporary relief. If you've lost market shares because competitors have higher quality products than you do, you can eliminate a thousand people, trim the budget by $10 million and still have inferior products.

No question, cost-cutting looks good to analysts. They'll praise your moves and announce your company has turned the corner. Don't be misled by their praise. Your quarterly "turn-around" will only last until the next quarter, or the one after that. You still haven't dealt with the elements of change that are far more powerful than the numbers on your balance sheet.

Some companies delude themselves. They assume that if they get "lean and mean," they've whipped their problems. It is a dangerous assumption. It can lead organizations down the wrong road; they throw all their resources into trimming the fat, ignoring the more substantive (and often more difficult) issues that confront the organization.

Remember: repositioning comes first, and financial turn-arounds follow. If you reverse the order, your financial turn-around is unlikely to last.

Repositioning Begins at Home

Successful repositioning begins within the corporation. You can't sell the outside world on something new until you sell your own people.

That means every employee, not just the executives at the top. Communicate what you plan to do and why you are doing it. Explain the plan, get everyone involved, make it exciting. You want your people looking forward to repositioning, not dreading it.

A company decides to revamp its customer service department. This means a new computer system, new forms to fill out, a reorganization of responsibilities and so on. Thousands of employees will be asked to learn a great deal in a short period of time and then implement what they've learned.

Imagine how difficult it will be to accomplish this repositioning if the majority of employees resent the revamp, or if they don't understand it, or if they're not motivated to learn and contribute.

Repositioning involves change, and change is threatening. A CEO's job is to remove the threat. Repositioning cannot be carried out in an atmosphere of intimidation and fear. The chief executive must make it his responsibility to inspire people to change. If he can use the carrot instead of the stick, even the most difficult repositioning can be undertaken.

One tactic worth considering is employee stock ownership plans. In repositioning situations, they provide employees with a stake in the repositioning's success. When you own a piece of the company, motivation comes naturally.

Two Words of Caution

When you begin your repositioning, don't fall into the trap of assigning responsibility to a long-term strategy group. Organizations will give such a group a fancy title and tell them to research the situation and come up with a report. After a number of months, the group presents its report.

And nothing happens! Why? It might be that the strategy group doesn't have access to the top executives in the corporation. Or it might be that their report becomes a political hot potato that no one wants to catch. Or it might be that the group's report is long on research and short on implementation; no one knows how to act on the group's findings.

Repositioning is too important for committees. The CEO should be in charge, and he should work with the managers most likely to put the repositioning into action.

Furthermore, don't think that you can buy a turnaround. Companies sometimes feel it's necessary to recruit fresh faces with fresh ideas in turnaround situations. There's nothing inherently wrong with that thinking. What's wrong is when these outsiders are paid substantially above the company's salary scale. The problem, of course, is that these overpaid outsiders create resentment among lesser-paid, long-term employees. It is difficult to work with someone—let alone to be motivated by them—when they are making twice your salary. Just as troubling, when the turnaround doesn't happen immediately, the higher-paid recruits are often scapegoated—they're the ones let go when organizations decide to trim the fat.

Spotlight Repositioning's Progress

Repositioning takes time—not just weeks or months, but years. During these years, you have to maintain your momentum. The repositioning effort that got off to such a grand start can flag if employees don't see their efforts bearing fruit.

Chart the progress of your repositioning in ways that everyone—not just the company's top executives—can see. New logos, packaging, advertising—all should be trumpeted and praised. Departments should be singled out for kudos when their efforts result in something tangible, something that advances the repositioning effort. Complimentary words from the boss, positive memos, and raises are just a few of the rewards that can be used.

At Spiegel, employees became celebrities when they moved us a little bit closer to our repositioning goal. When a buyer brought in an important new product line, she became a star—everyone congratulated her and she couldn't walk down the halls without someone telling her, ''Great job!''

The pride in accomplishing goals was everywhere. Even the product packers were proud and excited when we switched from brown paper packages to nice boxes with embossed logos.

We did everything possible to publicize our accomplishments. Don't be publicity-shy during a repositioning. Not only does publicity help reposition a company in its customers' eyes, but complimentary articles are savored by employees, especially when people in their departments are quoted or their efforts receive favorable mention.

Battling the Obsolete

In most instances, repositioning is a fight against obsolescence. Because the world is changing so rapidly and corporations have traditionally been slow to change, obsolescence is a constant enemy.

Technology might make a manufacturing process obsolete.

Shifts in population might cause a distribution system to become obsolete.

New consumer priorities might render a company's customer service methods obsolete.

It doesn't happen overnight. Obsolescence is evolutionary. You have to look at the big picture—to view things over time—or you won't be aware of the damage it does.

Study all facets of your corporation. Determine what parts are becoming obsolete. Attack the problem early. Remember, repositioning is easiest in the earliest stages of obsolescence.

If you reposition in a way that takes your company away from obsolescence, a turnaround will follow. Even if the situation seems dismal, it is likely that you can reposition successfully. Few companies are in worse shape than Spiegel was. Through our radical repositioning strategy, we turned the organization around. I don't want to make it sound easier than it was. To turn a huge corporation with thousands of employees in another direction requires an enormous effort. It took time, vigilance and inspiration, but we swung Spiegel company 180 degrees.

Don't underestimate the power of repositioning. Like any great idea, it can move mountains.

CHAPTER TWENTY-ONE

A Company's Soul

Culture is the difference between an organization and an institution, between a company with short-term goals and one with long-term visions. The right type of culture sustains a company, providing it with the bedrock values that enable it to survive the tough times and flourish during the good times.

Corporate culture is best defined through analogy. A corporation's tangible assets—its products, services, policies and people—are like a human body. They are functional and identifiable. A corporation's intangible assets—its philosophy, style of conducting business, attitudes toward employees—are its soul. Though these assets are not easily identifiable, they are no less valuable than tangible assets. They characterize the company's culture.

In the eighties, corporate cultures have been the subject of much discussion and debate. The raised awareness of the importance of culture is good. What's not good is the sizable number of organizations with inappropriate cultures. By inappropriate, I mean company cultures that prize profits over principles, a few key executives' rewards over fair compensation for the entire company, game playing and politics over ethical, humanistic ideals.

Companies with inappropriate cultures don't last. Oh, they might do fine for a while. If they have a terrific product or service and if they hit the market just right, they can sustain their success for months or even years. Ultimately, however, they will fail. They'll fail because they haven't sunk roots. They haven't established anything beyond the profit motive as the reason for their existence. Somewhere down the road, they'll encounter obstacles. When that happens, they'll have nothing to fall back on, no core vision that will give them the motivation and inspiration to tough it out.

Companies in this situation delude themselves. If success comes easily and quickly, they think that they don't require an ethical culture. They become arrogant, assuming that culture is irrelevant. They feel invulnerable, focusing on business strategy and tactics while ignoring deeper, more profound issues.

A culture must be cultivated. An organization that just gives the concept lip service, that writes a noble set of principles then stores it in a safe and forgets about it, will not have a viable, lasting culture. Actions are what determine culture.

The Dream Culture

Whatever a company's dream might be, it requires a supportive, synchronized culture.

For example, a food manufacturer decides to market a new line of products, all revolving around health-conscious alternatives to traditional snacks such as potato chips, pretzels and nuts. The company's dream is to revolutionize the way Americans snack, capitalizing on the growing evidence that salty and fried foods are unhealthy.

The company has been in business for years, marketing traditional snack foods. Their culture is marked by penny-pinching attitudes, encouragement of moderate risk-taking, a history of rewarding seniority with promotions and a strict adherence to rules and regulations.

It is not a bad culture. But it is also not one conducive to a dream strategy.

Dream strategies thrive in cultures of openness, flexibility, innovation and fairness. Attempting to change people's attitudes toward snacks is a bold plan, but it won't work if the culture isn't similarly bold. The first time the food company tries to run a groundbreaking ad campaign, the culture will kick in: The CEO will say, "This company can't do something that radical." The managers who are in charge because of seniority rather than ability won't implement the dream with sufficient imagination and initiative.

As you know from what took place at Spiegel, a corporate dream is driven by risk-taking, inspiration, motivation, leadership, communication and flexibility. If a company's underlying culture doesn't bring out these qualities, the dream won't enjoy an environment in which it can flourish.

Establishing and maintaining an appropriate culture for your dream strategy is a never-ending job. Unless a CEO and his policy makers give the job the importance it deserves, a culture can crumble.

The Erosion of Cultures

It is difficult to establish or maintain a solid culture in today's economic environment. The current emphasis on quarterly earnings combined with the rash of takeovers, mergers, leveraged buyouts and downsizing has played havoc with companies' values and principles.

How do you maintain an ethical, caring philosophy when you're the victim of an unfriendly takeover by a greedy, numbers-oriented company? How do you stick to your commitment of building an institution when securities analysts are keeping an eagle eye on your quarterly earnings?

Many organizations have given in to these pressures. I know of companies with terrific cultures that have been swallowed up by organizations with far different philosophies. The acquiring company imposes their values. They tell their new company,

"You've got to trim the fat," or "This is a cutthroat business, and the sooner you start squeezing for profits, the better."

Gradually, the acquired company assumes the culture of its new parent. As its people and policies give way to new ones, their values change.

Changing Cultures

Cultures can be changed, not only from good to bad but from bad to good.

When I arrived at Spiegel, the culture was one typical of a family-owned company. The Spiegel family's paternalistic approach to running a business had served them well for many years. Though there was nothing inherently wrong with their philosophy, the family culture was ill-suited to a highly competitive business. The contented, easy-going philosophy was neither motivational nor inspirational.

I changed the culture. The changes I implemented were different than the ones used to change the actual business and its image. Culture and image are two distinct things, and one should never be confused with the other (though one always affects the other).

I changed the culture through what I said and what I did. I expressed my firm belief in building a company that adhered to high moral standards, that prized risk-taking, that valued self-motivation and eschewed intimidation, that emphasized each employee's self-worth and believed that employees should be enthusiastic about what they do.

Specifically, if a subordinate made a mistake, I wouldn't chew her out unmercifully; I would explain why she made a mistake, but also give her the confidence and support so that she left my office feeling good about herself and her abilities.

I promoted people who deserved to be promoted. Politics and favoritism didn't enter into it. Everyone at Spiegel recognized that those who reaped the highest rewards contributed the most to the company's realization of its dream.

When we took a step forward or backward in pursuit of our dream, I let everyone know about it. I communicated our victories and defeats quickly and clearly. Subordinates weren't cut off from the information pipeline. I encouraged an open exchange of facts and ideas.

On many occasions, I insisted that Spiegel refuse to "milk" suppliers and customers. Even when times were tough, I refrained from putting pressure on our suppliers to lower their charges (if those charges were fair) or marking up our prices to customers above a reasonable level.

Over time, Spiegel's culture emerged. Like the outward reshaping of Spiegel, it didn't happen overnight. It took a while for my beliefs to sink in and spread, to be embraced by a growing number of employees.

In a way, changing a culture is even more difficult than changing a business strategy. The former is less tangible. It is similar to changing someone's religion, asking them to exchange one set of beliefs for another.

Take Your Culture Seriously

In the heat of battle, the culture often gets lost. You terminate a thirty-year employee without giving him the benefit of an early retirement program. You put pressure on a supplier to cut prices because the company has had a bad quarter. You introduce a product that doesn't meet your quality standards because you want to get your product out before a competitor's.

Who does it hurt? So what if you make a few exceptions?

The problem, of course, is that the exception can become the rule. Like a child who gets away with something once, you'll think you can get away with it again. But companies pay a price at some point in the future. As the culture disintegrates, so does the company's foundation.

Companies, like countries, should stand for something. Compare the United States to a dictatorship. This country espouses certain principles, as laid out by our founding fathers: democracy, equality, freedom of speech and so on. These principles influence our country's decisions, enabling us to pursue courses of action with conviction and certainty.

Dictatorships, on the other hand, have a different set of principles. They entail such things as consolidating power at the top, rigid control over the lives of its citizens, a lack of freedom, inequality.

Dictatorships tend to be brief, usually lasting no longer than the lifespan of the dictator.

Democracies endure.

Companies should examine their cultures and determine what principles dominate. Are greed, favoritism, power and intimidation distinguishing traits? If so, that culture probably won't sustain a company over the long run.

I'm not a purist. I recognize that mistakes will be made, that decisions will sometimes be at odds with the culture. Yet an organization should be aware of those mistakes and guard against repeating them.

Them That Gives, Gets

A strong sense of civic responsibility should be part of the culture. To ignore that responsibility is to ignore the mutually beneficial relationship between you and the marketplace: you should give back to society some of the financial largess that it has bestowed upon you.

This "payback" involves not only money and support for causes but active participation in good causes by members of your organization. An organization's CEO should take a leadership role in these endeavors.

A culture that fosters this community participation will be one with a real and compassionate belief in "giving back."

Dayton-Hudson, a Minneapolis retailer, is an excellent example of such a culture. For years, they've contributed 5 percent of profits to community betterment groups. So beloved is Dayton-Hudson that when the retailer was the target of takeover efforts, the entire state rallied around the company, helping Dayton-Hudson successfully fight off the sharks.

Culture Signs

Cultures manifest themselves in different ways. A company like IBM has a very formal culture, where employees adhere to clearly-defined rules and regulations. Another computer company has an informal culture, encouraging nonconformity in dress, attitudes and working hours.

Cultures shouldn't be judged on their outward manifestations. They should be judged on the positive or negative ways they affect employees. If a company's dress code is despised by employees, viewed as an example of the company's repressive mentality, then it is counterproductive. If employees consider a dress code to be an effective tool to apprise new hires of the organization's standards, then it's worthwhile.

Think about how your organization's employees perceive your culture and what their actions say about those perceptions. Do they spend a great deal of time currying favor with the people in power, thinking that playing politics is the single best way to advance their careers? Do they act as if showing enthusiasm and excitement is frowned upon? Do employees walk around glum-faced and dispirited, always looking over their shoulders to see who is watching them?

Though the principles that govern a culture are invisible, they have very real consequences. Every company has a personality, and employees try to conform their behavior to fit that personality. Employees "read" their organizations; it doesn't take long before they can sense what type of behavior is sanctioned, what styles of management are accepted.

213

Don't underestimate the importance of culture, even if you belong to a small company. Take a look at family-owned, one-product businesses that have flourished over many generations. It's not only their business strategy that has helped them do so well. It's their culture—a culture passed down from one generation to the next that encourages loyalty, honesty and compassion. It keeps morale high and relationships with customers and suppliers strong.

Cultural Satisfaction

What price success? What's the point of working for a business that achieves its goals through ruthlessness, chicanery and greed? I've always maintained that I never wanted to work for a company where winning came only with the devastation of competitors. Winning is not the only thing, and nice guys don't finish last.

The satisfaction comes from winning fairly and honestly. Whether you're the CEO or a mailroom worker, the joy is being part of a company whose values you can believe in.

At Spiegel, we built an institution. We created an organization that I hope will last long after I'm gone. It's not only the company that will endure, but the guiding principles we established. I have great faith that the Spiegel culture will survive, no matter how many changes the company will undergo in the future. That, more than anything else, makes the effort worthwhile.

CHAPTER TWENTY-TWO

A Dreamer and a Doer

You may already know much of what I've communicated. You may have already learned many of the lessons I've learned over the years. If you've been exposed to the world of business, I'm sure the knowledge I've shared with you is familiar.

But there's a big difference between knowing and doing. You have to put into action what you know.

To make sure you do so, I've created a list of questions. Consider the points listed, evaluating yourself not just once, but every day in every way. You will not only help your organization, but you will help yourself evolve as a manager and as a leader.

- Do I walk into work with a positive attitude, and am I happy there?
- Do I accept myself for who I am, and others for who they are?
- Do I carry out the work assigned me to the best of my ability?
- Do I add something of value to my work beyond what is expected of me?
- Do I try to understand my co-workers, subordinates and superiors better each day? Do I accommodate their personal traits and quirks?

- Do I understand the goals of the company?
- Do I recognize when the stated goals of the company aren't in line with how the company is operating? Do I set an example for others by my actions that I believe in those stated goals?
- Do I practice leadership qualities and show that I'm willing to be responsible and accountable?
- Do I accept my mistakes without being intimidated, and am I compassionate about the mistakes others make?
- Do I correct and criticize my subordinates and at the same time leave them with feelings of encouragement?
- Do I strive for promotions by improving myself, by executing my responsibilities properly so that I'll be the logical candidate for the job?
- Do I want to be a leader or am I satisfied with being a follower?
- Do I practice humanistic behavior, developing a perspective not only about my job, but about life?

If you can answer these questions affirmatively, anything is achievable. At Spiegel and throughout my career, I've relied on these questions to help me make the right decisions.

Since leaving Spiegel, I've encountered numerous challenges as a business consultant. I've been called on to help large and small companies, organizations in trouble and ones flush with prosperity. I've been involved in takeover battles, start-up strategies and crisis management situations.

Every consulting assignment has been different. But in each instance, my experience at Spiegel has proved invaluable. In my years there, I learned how a company can cope with change and come out on top. No matter how many obstacles are placed in a company's path by change, they can be overcome.

More than anything else, I hope this book has helped you confront the forces of change; to respond to the social, cultural, economic, ecological and technological forces reshaping the world.

How do you respond?

I can only tell you how I responded: with a dream. Call it what you will—a strategy, a vision, a great idea. No matter what term you use, it means taking the forces of change into consideration and creating a new approach. It means communicating your vision in a way that is inspirational and motivational. It means securing the enthusiastic support and belief of those who work with you.

If you're a chief executive, this is your chance to reshape an organization for the future. Instead of maintaining and preserving your company, you have the opportunity to lead it in a new direction.

Most of you, however, are not CEOs. You too can dream. If you're not in a position to lead your company, you can lead your division, your department, your group. You can find a way to make you and your people operate more efficiently, innovatively and effectively.

And all of you, even if you're the most junior executive, have a chance to contribute to your company's dream. Believe me, if you're with the right company, it will have a dream. If it doesn't, find one that does.

Contribute your ideas, your leadership. Do your part to move the company toward the dream's objectives. Use all your re- sources, intelligence, enthusiasm, initiative and talent to achieve the goal.

Every day and in every way, what you do says something about you and your organization. Don't let yourself or your organization down. Work as hard as you can to turn your dream into reality.

Don't be intimidated by failure. Every career and every com- pany has a history of mistakes. I've made my share of them, as did Spiegel. Live with them and learn from them. You'll be surprised at what you can accomplish. If you believe in a dream and work toward it's realization, the mistakes will be forgiven and forgotten, the successes rewarded and remembered.

HANK JOHNSON, as head of Spiegel, turned the near-bankrupt company into one of the leading catalog companies in the country. Mr. Johnson has been the subject of dozens of magazine articles and two video documentaries. In 1983, he received the Crain's Chicago Business "Executive of the Year" award. He was also named "Marketer of the Year" by the American Marketing Association. In 1985, the Horatio Alger Association of Distinguished Americans chose Hank Johnson as the winner of their Horatio Alger Award. He is currently a business consultant and lives in Downers Grove, Illinois.